I0888898

Praise for
Susan Ortolano and *Remarrying Right*:

"There aren't many books out there on this topic, and Susan has really opened the door to help those who are remarrying or remarried. Those divorce statistics are shocking for second and third marriages. I had no idea. I'm so glad there is a book like this to help people truly overcome obstacles, clear their pasts, and finally thrive in marriage."

Brett Dupree, Author of *Joyous Expansion: Unleash Your Passion to Lead an Inspired Life*

"Divorce completely changes the family structure, especially when you have kids involved. I believe the key to finding true love a second time around is to partner with an understanding best friend who appreciates and encourages spending quality time with your children even though the person is not the biological parent. With the critical information, tools, skills, and strategies that Susan presents in this book, finding love and having it last a lifetime actually feels reachable."

Patrick Snow, Publishing Coach and International Best-Selling Author of *Creating Your Own Destiny*

"As a formerly married woman, I always felt the playing field in the marriage game was not level. What I really needed on that field was a coach! Let Susan bring out the best in you... and your marriage."

Karen Jeffery, Author of
My Little French Diary

"Before taking the plunge again, dig down deep and read this powerful book. It reveals eye-opening truths and shares practical advice on how to make the right remarriage choice."

Susan Friedmann, CSP, International Best-Selling Author of
Riches in Niches: How to Make it BIG in a Small Market

"This book is not only great for couples getting married again but also for those who are getting married for the first time. The divorce rates are incredibly high, and if people had this knowledge and these skills in the first place, those high divorce rates would be so much lower. Bravo, Susan, for creating a book with critical information that can help make marriages exceptional and for extraordinary coaching."

Phyliss Francis-Wigfall, M.A., PCC, Business Coach,
Author of *Breaking Through Your Glass Ceiling*

"Susan's book reads like an important class on remarriage. She is a great teacher in all aspects, and this book is a powerful opportunity to learn about marriage, remarriage, and how to create one that lasts a lifetime. I resonated with it so much!"

Anne Reinhard, Teacher and Writer

"This book means so much to me. I was a widow with children and didn't know if I would marry again as my priority was caring for my sons. I did meet and marry a wonderful man, and while we have been married for a while with a blended family, the tools and information in this book have been so helpful. Thank you, Susan, for writing this book!"

Lisa Morgenstern, Speech Therapist

"I never really believed in the concept of a soul mate, but I believe in it the way Susan describes it and am happy to be with mine. This book can help so many couples regardless of whether it's their first, second, or even third marriage! It's a must have for all married couples and I look forward to reading future books by Susan!"

Lynn Peters, Relationship Coach

"Susan Ortolano really has her heart on the pulse of what it takes to succeed in marriage after experiencing a painful divorce. I hope all remarried couples read this book, do the exercises, and take their remarriage to a new level. There isn't a lot of material out there for remarriage, so Susan's book will help so many people. I was stunned to see that divorce rates are even higher for second and third marriages. There is fantastic education and information provided in these pages!"

Michelle Benson, Teacher

"If they only taught some of this material in school, the divorce rates would be so much lower. Everyone wants love in their lives and most want love that lasts forever. This gem of a book truly lights the way for couples to enter marriage again."

Danielle Crayton, Teacher

"I can't tell you how helpful this book can be for couples getting remarried. Susan's insights and practical skills and tools can help couples approach their next marriage in a new way."

Michael Franks, CPA

"*Remarrying Right* definitely addresses issues that come up in remarriage, but also in any marriage. I would recommend this book to anyone who is married, has been married, or has remarried. Read it, do the exercises provided, and learn!"

Ben Carragan, Clinical Psychologist

"Susan is an extraordinary Relationship Coach with an extra dose of intuition! She has helped me for many years from getting through dating again after being a young widow to working with issues that have come up in my second marriage. Susan is truly gifted and her book is incredibly helpful!"

Lana Voring, Marriage Family Therapist

"I not only love this book, but I adore working with Susan! I have been stuck in how to move forward in my third marriage, and I thought I might be getting divorced again, but reading this book and receiving coaching from Susan has literally saved me from another trip to divorce court!"

Callie Morton, Graphic Designer

"Susan Ortolano brings passion, humor, and critical information about marriage and relationships. She speaks in a very compassionate and personable style!"

Mary Kathryn Holbrook, Relationship Expert

"Susan is the most gifted relationship coach I know. She is amazing at what she does, and even before we were married, she coached me and did intuitive readings for me to help me find my second (and forever) wife. She had no idea at the time that it would be her, but it has been a privilege and a blessing to be married to her with all of the knowledge, insights, intuition, and skills she has. She is a beautiful person inside and out, and she takes a personal, humorous, down-to-earth, and compassionate approach to helping people transform their relationships. She certainly has transformed mine, and my life. You may think I 'should' say all of those things, being her husband, but she is truly extraordinary and is the real deal!"

Rick Ortolano, M.A.
Hospice Chaplain
Susan's Second and Forever Husband!

"Isn't love the most important area of life? Getting marriage right was my dream. Getting divorced wasn't, but getting remarried has been great, and Susan's book, along with her masterful coaching, has helped me tremendously! I can't thank her enough!"

Marnee Guastram, Teacher

"Susan is a fantastic Relationship Coach and Marriage Mentor. As a man who has been married before it has been important for me to make this marriage the one that lasts. Susan's book along with her incredible coaching has supported me through this important process."

Joseph A. Wigfall II, CLC, Certified Life & Leadership
Coach, Author of *Becoming The Empowered Leader*

My soul has been crushed, my heart has been torn,

I've been through this before, but will no longer mourn.

Ravaged by tears and anger I'd never known,

After the last marriage was destroyed,
I swore I'd go it alone.

But love beckoned me fiercely and
my heart opened once more,

I felt a strong yearning to go back and explore.

So with new strength, I embrace it again,

And to this next marriage path, I commit 'til the end.

Let me show you the way….

— Susan Ortolano

REMARRYING RIGHT

CREATING
EVERLASTING
LOVE WITH YOUR
TRUE SOUL MATE

SUSAN ORTOLANO, M.A.

PUBLISHING
New York

Remarrying Right
Creating Everlasting Love With Your True Soul Mate

Published by:
Aviva Publishing
Lake Placid, New York
(538)-523-1320

Address all inquiries to:

Susan Ortolano
Telephone: 818-232-3186
Email: susan@conscioussoulmates.com
www.remarryingright.com
www.conscioussoulmates.com

ISBN: 978-1-943164-45-5

Library of Congress: 2015918005

Editor: Tyler Tichelaar, Ph.D.
Cover Design: Nicole Gabriel/Angel Dog Productions
Interior Book Layout: Nicole Gabriel/Angel Dog Productions
Author Photo: Savannah Furry, Nicole Gabriel

Every attempt has been made to source properly all quotes.

Printed in the United States of America

First Edition

2 4 6 8 10 12

I dedicate this book to my second (and forever) husband,
Rick Ortolano.

You are the love of my life and have shown me what everlasting love with my true Soul Mate is all about. Thank you for supporting me, believing in me, accepting me for the nutty gal that I am, for making me laugh when I want to cry, for crying with me when my own tears are falling, for sharing with me and writing with me thousands of the most beautiful words I could ever read or hear. Thank you for marrying me when you knew I had serious medical issues and for walking that journey with me. You have loved me and held me through heartbreaking moments and exciting breakthroughs. I love you for challenging me to keep evolving and growing personally and spiritually, and for telling me how beautiful I am through your eyes, even with Kleenex shoved up my nose and Vick's VapoRub smothered over my chest during the yuckiest flu I had had in years. You have shown me what true loving connection, compassion, and wisdom look like with that amazing heart of yours, and what a blessed and treasured gift marriage is. I thank you for making my marriage dreams come true. I love and appreciate you with all my heart and am one blessed lady to know that I am somebody's dream and that we hold each other's hands walking the path of marriage together.

And

To my parents, Bob Block and Barbara Cope.

Thank you for showing me that divorce is not a shameful scarlet letter, nor the end of the world, that parents with kids can divorce without putting each other down, as well as wish the best for each other, regardless of their union splitting apart. I thank you for modeling how important it is to choose the right partner, and how remarriage can be a lifelong blessing.

**Marriage is the mosaic you build with your spouse.
Millions of tiny moments that create your love story.**

— *Jennifer Smith*

ACKNOWLEDGMENTS

I want to start by acknowledging Rick Ortolano for being the love of my life and for his eternal belief in me.

To Phyliss Francis-Wigfall, Anne Reinhard, Gabrielle Whitney, Bess Kaufman, Lisa Morgenstern, Debbie Montes, Sue Seely, Crystle Horner, and Kate Duggan for being my go-to gals and dearest friends.

To the Reinhard/Vallejo family for being my God-family.

To the Francis/Wigfall family for your mutual support and allowing me to feel like part of your family.

To Ryan Simmons for being my "brother-son" and allowing me to work some mommy muscles I never got to use, and to Kari Rose Simmons for being my Yankee doodle "sister-daughter."

To Brenda Zeller for being my amazing team captain extraordinaire, right-hand gal, and dear friend.

To Patrick Snow for being my magnificent book mentor and coach for life, along with his talented fiancée Nicole Gabriel for making me, my book, and my materials look so beautiful.

To the extraordinary Brian Whetten for being a friend, a colleague, a coach, and a mentor, and for allowing me to support him.

To the brilliant coaches and practitioners I have worked with for inspiring and generous coaching, specifically Nicholas Rave for "seeing me" and helping me choose this niche as a specialty, as it is also my story.

To my mentor coach, Sheri Boone, whose coaching skills blow me away.

To Christy Jacobs for keeping my hopes alive and being the real deal.

To Valerie Harrell, Joanne Mednick, Anita Bains, Rob Krochmal, David Jernigan, and David Jowdy, for their amazing contributions to my life.

To Frankie Doiron for her support and sharing in the commitment to training other relationship coaches.

To the late Rob Huston for his years of service and volunteering to assist me in training other couples' coaches. We miss you, buddy!

To my dear friend "Cuach" for reminding me how to have courage and strength in the face of darkness.

To my teachers, practitioners, and medical masters who have taught, inspired, and supported me.

To my editor, Tyler Tichelaar, for turning my big rambling run-on sentences into a coherent flow of a book.

To my own family: Barbara and Lee Cope, Bob Block and Sue Barkhurst-Block, David and Marcia Block, Maya Block, Dani

Block, the late Papa Nick Ortolano, the late Mary Ortolano, and my own blended family bonus siblings, Sarah, David & Kristin, Stacy & Scott, and Dwayne & Wendy and their families.

To those of you who are reading this, thank you for not just picking up another book but for caring enough about having a successful marriage to do so. You are the inspiration for all of this.

And finally, to the many singles, individuals, and couples who have given me the privilege of being their coach and clairvoyant, you all know who you are, and I'm so grateful for all of you.

Disclaimer: Examples of couples mentioned in this book are fictional or a composite of multiple different couples. In all cases, names and other information have been changed to protect individuals' privacy.

THE FIFTEEN ESSENTIAL INGREDIENTS

In this book, I have shared fifteen essential ingredients for Remarrying Right. While it may sound like a lot, you may find it more easy to integrate than you might think. These are not necessarily ingredients that follow in a particular order like adding eggs before flour or chocolate chips after sugar. These are essential ingredients that will help guide you to make your marriage grow, evolve, and thrive with harmony, fun, passion, and new levels of understanding. There is a first ingredient for those who are single again to get back in the game following the loss of a marriage. This ingredient will help them to find the mate for their soul that leads them to walk the journey of marriage again. Divorced singles who want to remarry can't really skip that one, as much as fear may come up even thinking about it. The other ingredients are more ongoing and meant to be infused into the day-to-day life of the marriage and integrated on a more regular basis. Keep these ingredients in mind and practice using the skills you learn from them as you, as a couple, move forward together. For those about to start this next path of remarriage, study them and start using them now. Be mindful and take good care of this marriage by using these ingredients like they are part of a recipe for forever that depends on this very specific mixture; then you will have what you need to make this marriage last a lifetime!

CONTENTS

Preface

HOW TO GET THE MOST OUT OF THIS BOOK

Thank you for choosing to read this book! It is designed to provide you with information and education on the right ingredients to remarry right. Whether you are remarrying, already remarried, divorced and wanting to marry again, or in a first marriage but want to have new insights, be inspired, and learn new skills, these are the ingredients for you.

Each chapter has key information about marriage and remarriage, examples and stories of real couples, including stories from my own life, and exercises that will allow you to reflect upon and apply the information so you can create and nurture your relationship with your future spouse and fully transform both of you into the couple you desire. My recommendation for couples reading this book is for each of you to have your own copy so you can individually complete the exercises for yourself. They can be done together, but it is more effective if you each have your own copy to reflect upon and write in.

Yes, there are exercises, so this book doubles as a workbook to give you extra value.

I want to encourage you to dig deeply into the exercises, carry this book with you, and really dive into the growth and transformational experiences available for you and your marriage.

So this is an opportunity not just to read yet another book on "how to do marriage again," but to learn and experience your unique path, whether it's for your upcoming remarriage or the remarriage you are already in. By working both individually and together through these pages, you will experience greater love, deepen your partnership, gracefully resolve issues, and evolve together! Marriage is one of the greatest teachers as it is guaranteed to bring up old wounds and old "stories" for you to heal. With the right partner, it is a beautiful opportunity for a wonderful journey together and also an opportunity to grow and heal. So I like to say that if you aren't going to be a monk on a mountain learning to become an enlightened being, be in a marriage because it will be one of your greatest teachers.

Embrace the journey!

Introduction

REFUSING TO THROW IN THE MATRIMONY TOWEL

"Once you believe you are worthy of love,
you'll never settle for anyone's second best treatment."

— Charles J. Orlando

As a child, did you ever dream of growing up, getting married to someone you loved, having beautiful children, and then after a few years, getting a divorce? Yeah, me neither, but there I was, thirty-three years old, signing divorce papers after eight years of being with my first husband and over five years of being married to him. (Yes, I was counting.) Eight years with him felt like I was doing hard time in some prison, but I sadly realized it was a prison of my own making rather than the sappy Hallmark movie I had hoped for.

As I signed the divorce papers, I felt both a sense of relief and an alarming fear about what the future would bring for me. I had spent the majority of those eight years walking on eggshells, living in constant fear while my soon to be former husband had spent those years lying, cheating, being verbally abusive toward me, disappearing at all hours of the day and night, and often being unemployed because he didn't "feel" like working, putting a financial burden on me that I did not ask for. He had never given me even so much as a card on my birthday or on holidays, much less a gift. During the first few years, he had not brought in any money to our household. I had even had to buy my own wedding ring for our ceremony and just got something to have on my ring finger. Later, I bought a nicer wedding ring set for myself as my then husband didn't feel like doing that either. I could go on and share more "war stories," but you get the point.

My marriage experience had rocked me to the core, bringing up a lot of self-worth, rejection, self-esteem, and value issues within me. Imagining my future, I now feared I would never find anyone who would really love, cherish, and be faithful to me. My former husband's parting "gift" to me was an unexpected STD, proving to me that I had absolutely made the right decision to request a divorce.

I was relieved to move on, but I definitely had some major adjusting to do, internally and externally. I was left wondering why all of this had happened...*again.* After all, it hadn't been the first time I had been with a man who had treated me poorly, cheated, or lied, and I intended it to be the last time. Fortunately, I hadn't been married to the others, but the pain of all these experiences jolted me in a similar way.

Stepping back out on my own was both exciting and scary. I had grown accustomed to having a husband around (well, at least some of the time), saying to people that I was married, and being called "Mrs." I wondered what living on my own again as a single woman and navigating the world of dating would be like. The thought of dating again made me cringe. I was no longer twenty-five, and while I wasn't quite a "troll" in the appearance department, I wasn't a super model either. I had some wobbly bits, couldn't have biological children, had some health issues, and wondered who in the world would even be interested in me. As you can see, I also had some internal self-confidence work to do!

I did date another guy soon after my divorce. I even had a two-and-a-half-year relationship with a man, who was very kind but didn't seem to love me quite enough and consistently questioned our union while I tried to talk him into loving me. I'm not sure it was the right fit for either of us, but because we were both kind people, we carried on. We were even engaged (I talked him into it) until we both knew it just wasn't going to work. There was no shattering destructive event; we were just two good people who made great friends, but not a suitable match for marriage. I still believed at that time that I had to convince someone to love me so deciding to break up and start again, while scary, was actually a powerful moment for me as I felt some strength gather up within me and some internal changes about to burst wide open, but I didn't know quite what they were yet.

I felt very lost and confused in this world of relationships, but

I knew I had to do something about it after it hit me that I was the common denominator in my sea of similar relationships. Those changes ready to burst had everything to do with that and I knew something internal had to shift in order for that change to burst wide open.

I did understand the value of marriage and had a strong intention to be a happily married woman. My father (with good intentions) had told me to prepare to be a stepmother. After all, I was in my mid-thirties at that point, so the men I would likely meet would be divorced with children. Since I wasn't able to have children, I had to let go of the idea that I would be a mom. I felt adoption could be on the table, and since I had been a teacher, I knew I could care for other people's children, so I was clear I could love an adopted child. I had also been a stepdaughter for more than half my life, so I had the experience that blended families could be both beneficial and complex. Adoption seemed complicated, so I was really hoping to meet and marry a man who didn't have children from a previous marriage, yet my father's words, warning me to prepare myself for being a stepmother, stuck with me.

Fortunately, through a lot of personal growth work, and some amazing mentors, I figured it out for myself. The internal shifts were happening, and I realized what had made me fall into the trap of what I call "the karma marriage." It's the marriage or long-term relationship that really shows us what we need to shift internally. It projects right at us all of our inner stories and beliefs about ourselves as if we are watching a sad movie on a huge movie screen. That experience has inspired me to share what I have learned with you.

INTRODUCTION

Are you experiencing challenges in your second or third marriage? Are you divorced and afraid to get back out there again? Are you noticing issues from the past starting to show up? Have you truly healed the ghosts of marriage(s) past? Have you healed the programming that was unintentionally instilled during your early years in your family of origin?

Today, as I write this, I have become the happily married woman I always dreamed of being. I have been married to the most amazing man, Rick, since 2001, and he is everything I had hoped and wished for, plus much more. He is kind, compassionate, loving, and affectionate. He knows how to love me. I am showered with beautiful cards, words of love, affirmations, compliments, and amazing love and incredible care. We are very much aligned in our core values, relationship requirements (must haves), core essential needs, and shared interests, making us very compatible. He even cooks for me! And while he was previously married, he and his first wife did not have children either, so we were perfect for each other.

Everything about this relationship just felt right at a deep levels, and I know I remarried right this time. Sometimes, I wonder how the hell it happened, but I learned what I needed and what most people need.

This book is for those of you who have been married before and are either looking to get back out there, about to get married again, or are in a second or third marriage. This book is also for you if you married someone who has been married before, even if it's your first marriage. If it is your first marriage and you've married someone who has been divorced, you have still likely gone through some long-term relationships, possibly lived with someone, or maybe even been engaged. The tools and transformational information in this book will support you as well. This book explains the challenges of remarriage and teaches the tools required and ingredients necessary to make your next relationship amazing and to know truly how to be remarried right.

You can do the exercises on your own or with your partner, but I encourage you to work on them together or at least share together. This process will be an education like nothing you were ever taught in school! Can you imagine if schools did teach about relationships, how much better off the world would be? I did have the opportunity to do that when I taught High School for a while until budget cuts happened. I could go on forever about that topic, but just know that much of what I share in this book can be applied to other relationships in your life, including those with your parents, siblings, friends, coworkers, perhaps even your pets. Any efforts you make to improve any relationships can only be beneficial in the end.

The personal story I will share throughout these pages is just a small part of my experiences being married, divorced, and married again. I have spared the reader many details of my first marriage because they would make most people cringe. The path I took to create the transformation and success in my second marriage is what is more important to focus upon so you can learn from it. There are other stories as well from clients I have worked with that I know you will relate to and learn from. My wish is that you know you are not alone on this journey.

The Use of the Term "Soul Mate"

I can easily say I have found my true soul mate, but what does that actually mean? In our culture, a soul mate is generally defined as the one person you are meant to spend your life with. I believe the term soul mate means "the mate who aligns with your soul," or "the mate who connects with you at a soul level." I believe we have several "contenders" to fit what I call our own soul mate "suit." The soul mate suit is comprised of everything we have ever wanted in a spouse. We alter the suit as we grow and evolve, meaning the person who fit the suit the first time, may not have grown with it, or couldn't stay in it for whatever reason. What we can do is create everlasting love with our true soul mate, the spouse we choose to walk the journey of marriage with as we gain more clarity about our soul mate suit and the person who fits it best. For those of you who thought your previous spouse was your soul mate, just know that at the time, he or she actually may have been, but when the growth happened, the suit no longer fit. Our goal is to remarry right, meaning remarry for the right reasons, with the right skills, because it feels right at a deep level, and because we know that the person we marry is right for us, a soul mate, a person who connects with us on a soul level in all areas of marriage.

Since the divorce statistics are even higher for second and third marriages (60-90 percent! Whoa!), I hope this book offers you the ingredients you need to prepare for your marriage or to build or rebuild it into something beautiful with your true soul mate so you may walk the path of love together forever.

The Use of the Term *"Right"*

While the title of this book is *Remarrying Right*, I wanted to share what that means. There is no one "right" way to be in a marriage, but there are ways to be in a marriage that work and some that do not work. Most of you have experienced the latter, and stepping forward into a new marriage and getting it "right" means coming into it with a higher level of awareness, again, a better set of relationship skills, a greater sense of love for yourself, tools to help let go of the past, a consciousness or mindset that has evolved, and tools to stay connected and communicate well. Remarrying Right is also about making sure you are with someone you align with and share core values with who meets your own relationship criteria. It is also about who you are and the sense of love and wholeness you bring to the partnership. As you read the book and do the exercises, you will have a greater understanding of what "right" means to you because "right" at its core is what is right for you.

Chapter 1

EXPLORING SOME MYTHS AND CHALLENGES OF REMARRIAGE

"I have found the one whom my soul loves."

— Author Unknown

Sorting Through a Few Myths about Remarriage

What have you heard out in the world about remarriage? What have you heard about what it takes to have a successful one? Many myths about getting remarried, both positive and negative, exist. I encourage you not to believe the myths as much as your own direct experience, but do pay attention to tips and tools from marriage experts or couples who have been successful at remarriage. Take everyone's feedback into account, sort it through for yourself; review the feedback you have gathered here, in this book, and through other books or qualified sources, and notice what resonates and aligns with you and who you are as an individual and as a couple and then apply it. In this first chapter, we will look at some of the myths and challenges you may be sorting through about being married again from my point of view as a professional relationship and marriage coach and from my own experience being in a successful second marriage. See if you can recognize anything here that you believe or have experienced.

- One myth about remarriage is that being with a new and different person means you will automatically have a new and better marriage experience. While there is some truth to that, you are going to *carry* your past with you internally until it gets healed or cleared to a specific degree, so I guarantee you it will be projected or reflected back at you through this new marriage if it is not processed or healed. The more you heal and clear, the better your remarriage experience will be. An example is if you had poor communication in your first marriage, those missing skills will carry over into your second one. Not only that—you may attract or have attracted someone with poor communication skills.

- Another myth about remarriage is that you are now older, wiser, more established, and have already had a marriage experience; therefore, you now know better. It's true you did learn a lot through that experience, but what you had before didn't really work, so just being older, wiser, and more experienced doesn't, in and of itself, spare you from needing new skills and tools to have a better and long-lasting marriage experience. Since we are not really taught how to have a great marriage in school, we just follow along with what we interpret from witnessing the marriages or lack thereof of our family of origin—parents, grandparents, aunts, and uncles—and then we absorb that energy. We also again look at the culture, what television marriage and movie marriage looks like, and we often expect it to be that way.

- An additional myth about remarriage is that it attaches a stigma to you, like a scarlet letter of failure, guilt, shame, and some kind of stamp on your head that something is wrong with you. Perhaps that was more common forty years ago, but in this day and age, while that may happen in some religions or cultures, the reality can be seen in the statistics. You are not alone in your experience of having a marriage that did not last. Given the high divorce rate statistics for first marriages, while some people are gun-shy about getting married again, there is no need to place the scarlet letter of failure on yourself. This is a new opportunity for you to heal, to learn to receive love, and to experience joy and happiness at its best with someone who is right for you. So if you have that feeling of failure inside, or you feel you are walking with the myth that there is stigma attached to you, feel free to let that go.

- Another myth about remarriage is that there is an easy out. If this doesn't work out, let's face it, you have either been divorced or lost a spouse before, and while it was very painful, you survived. And while it would be awful to go through that more than once, you know you could survive it again. However, you already know that losing a marriage is a very steep fall, so the myth that it's easy to step out of one is like saying, "Let's have another child because giving birth wasn't that painful." It's painful! I know that having babies is worth the pain, but divorce isn't. Divorce is painful, loss is painful, and the idea that you can take the commitment lightly, perhaps with one foot out the door because you can survive the downfall easily is a myth. That downfall would compound the pain of the original loss, and if there are children involved, it can be even more painful and confusing for them. You then would have two former spouses, which makes marriage an even more challenging institution to commit to.

- Then we have the Brady Bunch myth. Raising children is a beautiful yet complex journey. Since almost half of remarriages involve children, many think bringing their children and mixing them with the children of the next spouse is going to look like the family on *The Brady Bunch*. Everyone will get along so well that you will be one big happy, peaceful, loving, conflict-free family. You may even get Alice as your live-in housekeeper. Blended families are not always a Brady Bunch experience. Many issues can affect children from divorced families and those issues are brought forward into a blended family. In this book, we will explore some of those challenges and dispel the myth. That doesn't mean a family can't blend well together, but it is not an automatic, easy process.

Those are just a few myths, just the tip of the iceberg. Let's now dive into some of these challenges and myths in detail so you have the understanding, tools, knowledge, and skills necessary to make your new marriage amazing.

Sifting Through Some of the Challenges of Remarriage

When I was a little girl, I believed the fairy tale about happily-ever-after, so I never imagined I would be married more than once. I don't think many people dream of being married multiple times. My own parents divorced when I was nine, modeling for me that divorce happens. I don't remember them fighting much. I don't remember any warning signs that they would split up. It seemed like everything happened all of a sudden. One day, my father sat me down and explained that he and my mother just didn't love each other anymore. He let me know that he was going to take my brother on a trip for the "Indian Guides" group they were in together and then go on a two-week vacation. And then I remember that all of a sudden he had moved elsewhere. I don't recall a speech about that. I don't recall the day he moved out. I just remember that one day he no longer lived with us. He did have us help him set up his new place, but the transition part seemed to happen so fast.

As an adult, I now know more about the issues my parents had in their marriage and why they divorced. They are now both happily remarried and have been with their respective spouses for over thirty years.

While they have remained friendly with each other and inclusive with my brother, my step-siblings, and all of the grandkids, they have also had successful second marriages that have gone the long haul. The people they married had been divorced with children as well, so I have been a part of two blended families since I was fourteen.

Just before my fiftieth birthday, I found out even more about why my parents' marriage to one another didn't last (Thanks, Mom!), and as a middle-aged, trained relationship coach and a woman in a successful second marriage, I totally understood more of what happened. The adult in me absolutely understood. The younger and adolescent girl in me was still healing layers of the "post child of divorce" experience, which wasn't about the divorce itself—it was about what happened afterwards. As a woman who is in a successful second marriage, it was modeled for me that a second marriage could be incredibly rewarding, successful, and joyful. So when I was deciding whether to get a divorce from my first husband, while stewing over my future, I made a decision with an understanding that there could be a better and more aligned spouse for me.

For the remainder of this chapter, let's look in detail at three of the biggest challenges that face a remarriage:

1. The challenge of a blended family
2. The challenge of letting go of the past
3. The challenges faced by being widowed vs. divorced when remarrying

1) The Challenge of a Blended Family

Earlier, I mentioned the Brady Bunch myth and that blended families can be rewarding and add richness and love to our lives. Are there challenges with blended families? Yes. In fact, statistics say that 40 percent of second marriages include children from the previous marriage. Blended families can be part of a major challenge when a second or third marriage includes children, even grown ones. It is not easy for kids to see their parents divorce, and it is not easy to see them dating or being with another spouse. How kids cope following those experiences depends on how the parents handle the process and how they handle their relationship as co-parents in addition to their relationship with each other. Also, the ages of children when their parents divorce or remarry, and the relationship that develops with the soon-to-be or existing stepparent makes a huge impact on the family dynamics. Other issues in a blended family that this book will address are circumstances like holidays, visitation, co-parenting with former spouses, finding time for the new marriage, and finances, including child support, alimony, etc.

My parents handled things as best as they could while going through their divorce. Following the divorce, they were trying to figure out their own lives and to discover themselves along with their true dreams in life and in love. While that was a necessary process for them, my brother and I got somewhat lost in the shuffle, being left basically to care for ourselves. We were provided for, yes, but our parents were exploring life again as individuals, and that exploration didn't always include their kids. Balancing time with kids and learning how to have a relationship with step-kids is highly essential. There is so much more to be accountable for, to nurture, and to integrate. It is not always a graceful and easy balance or transition for kids, parents, or stepparents, but we will look more into how best to create that balance later in this book.

2) The Challenge of Letting Go of the Past

We will dive fully into this challenge later as well, but for now, here are a few aspects to consider:

- It is crucial to have complete closure with the romantic relationship with your former spouse. If you are co-parenting, make it a positive co-parenting experience. If you feel incomplete and tempted to stay in a romantic, flirty, and ultra-sentimental space with your former spouse, you will do major damage to your current marriage.

- It is essential to let go of your past. Part of letting go of the past is letting go of your internal stories, beliefs, and issues of the past as well. If you don't work on this, the person you have attracted for your remarriage will likely resemble the person you're trying to leave behind, so your marriage could become a carbon-copy of the last one. Basically, you can't run and you can't hide from yourself. If you try, your external reality will reflect what has not been healed, cleared, or completed internally. We will address some helpful techniques for letting go later in the book.

- It is fine to feel confident, but it's dangerous to think you don't have more to learn or don't need to grow. Feeling overconfident with thoughts such as, "Hey, I've done this; I've got this" can block you from being open to the new skills and tools you need to create a successful remarriage. There are new skills, tools, and much more to learn to start a successful marriage. Doing what you did the first time doesn't make a second marriage successful. It just means you may be repeating what didn't work the first time.

- Managing money in a remarriage is definitely a hot topic! It can be a great challenge because you are coming into or came into this marriage in a different financial position than you did the first time. We will delve into this subject in a future chapter, but when you consider that one or both of you may bring assets from your own achievements and have children that you planned to support with those assets, money has to be handled consciously. It can be a huge challenge if this area is not discussed and planned for carefully.

- As I mentioned before, many people feel like they can survive another divorce if need be. This again

> brings forward a challenge to the level of commitment people choose to make in a remarriage. A weaker level of commitment is one reason for the higher divorce rate for second and third marriages. It is critical to commit fully to this marriage and not leave one foot out the door. Believing there is an escape hatch doesn't help a marriage succeed. Obviously, leaving is appropriate under certain circumstances, but fully committing is very important to the marriage's duration and quality.

I worked with a couple that had some of the financial issues I mentioned. He was a multi-millionaire, but she was newer to her career so she hadn't made that kind of money. He was fiercely controlling and protective of *his* money, so he tried to control their finances and her access to them. She was left having very little idea of their financial situation. While his wife benefitted from his financial status, she also felt controlled by it. She didn't feel she had a voice in a lot of the decision-making because he was the one with the big bucks. He didn't want to merge their finances either, and he made her sign a strong pre-nuptial agreement. He made sure he was protected and that she would get very little in the event of a divorce. She wasn't planning for a divorce, so she was not concerned and did not stipulate what she would be entitled to if they did split up. He also took control of her income when she was working since, initially, she felt comfortable combining their finances. Then they bought a new home, and she had to fight to have her name on the title.

The husband in this marriage definitely had trust issues that carried over from his first marriage, and money was the major area of mistrust for him. He wasn't willing to work on these issues so they caused major conflict. After six years, when she found out her husband had been unfaithful, the couple divorced. She didn't get much of a settlement due to the pre-nuptial agreement. She had been laid off from her job a few years prior and was working on creating a business for herself that hadn't taken off yet. She left the marriage with her clothes, her car, some furniture, and a year's worth of alimony. Some might say that was a really great settlement, but for her, it was tough. While money wasn't the main reason their second marriage didn't work, it was an issue that continued to come up in their marriage.

Most couples with challenges have an opportunity to find common ground where both partners feel a negotiated "win" exists. So know that most of the challenges faced have a solution. You don't have to let your past marriage and situations from it affect your current marriage. We'll look at how to avoid this situation in more detail later.

3) The Challenge of Being Divorced vs. Being Widowed

While divorce and being widowed both create a profound sense of loss and challenges moving forward, being widowed and remarrying vs. being divorced and remarrying are two very distinct experiences. I don't bring up this topic to compare who suffers more, but to express that what has happened in past relationships and the way we store it inside us will be carried forward into the next marriage.

Many who divorce *choose* to do so. Many divorced people also may never want to connect with their former spouse again. If they have children, however, they need to co-parent despite not wanting that contact. By comparison, people who are widowed did not make that choice, and most of them deeply miss their spouses. Their pain is based in a deeper level of grief while divorced people more likely feel more anger or regret about their past marriage.

Because I cannot speak directly to the experience of being widowed and remarrying, I will share the perspective of a client who underwent that experience. She is now remarried and a stepmother to three children while also having two of her own biological children from her first marriage. Her second husband was divorced. Here is their story and the challenges they have faced:

It was a beautiful, bright, sunny perfect California day. Leah and Adam had been happily together for many years, since their early twenties. They had a beautiful two-year-old son and a baby on the way. Leah was walking her little guy on that perfect California day, feeling peaceful and happy about the fact that her new baby was going to arrive in a few months. She had no idea what was about to happen.

Leah and her son had just gotten home and settled when she suddenly heard a shaking noise coming from the master bedroom. At first, she thought it was an earthquake, but then she realized nothing else was shaking. She ran upstairs to where Adam had been resting. The moment she saw him, she recognized that he was in the midst of a grand mal seizure.

After getting Adam to the hospital via ambulance, several tests were done and a mass was found on his brain. Leah was shocked, numb, and devastated. They both immediately jumped into treatment options and action mode to see what could be done. Surgery, chemo, and radiation followed, but the mass was so aggressive that soon they received the horrifying news that nothing was working.

Their second child was born in the midst of this nightmare. What should have been a beautiful time to nest with the children was transformed into a transition period of helping Adam through the process of dying. Ten months following the birth of their second child, Adam passed way, leaving Leah to care for a three year old and a ten month old on her own. She was in her early thirties and had never imagined she would end up being a single working mom raising two small boys. While she had help from family and friends, for a very long while, all she could manage were the daily functions of caring for her two children and going to work. Her life as she knew it was never going to be the same. She was widowed, scared, and deeply grieving. She could only move forward by taking small steps at a slow pace. It took several years before she was ready to date again, and she wanted to make sure her two children were a bit older before she did. After she began dating and exploring what she wanted, she finally met Ethan, the man she remarried.

Leah said she will never forget Adam. She sees his face and mannerisms in her two sons, but she has had to put her memory of their life together in a box with a beautiful bow, knowing that it is part of her past, and meeting and marrying Ethan was her present and future.

Ethan, on the other hand, had been married and divorced after being betrayed by his wife through infidelity. He felt embarrassed, shamed, and betrayed. It all hit his self-esteem in a very deep way. It was hard to move forward. He and his wife did not part ways in a friendly manner, and no matter what he did to try to keep things amicable, she continued to be manipulative, angry, and mean toward him. They had three young children at the time, so he had to continue a relationship with her for the children's sake, which made moving forward tough for him.

So Ethan and Leah met, dated, fell in love, brought their children together, and got remarried. While they became a blended family, it is clear that both of them carried forward wounds from their past experiences into their new marriage. Ethan had previously been cheated on and had a lot of trust issues to sort through. Leah, having lost her first husband, had some additional deep healing to do. They thought their children would blend well together immediately, but blending the family became a challenge as each of the five children had his or her own wounds to heal. They would withdraw, act out, and disrespect their stepparent. They would also loudly express anger, resentment, and sadness. Leah and Ethan had a hard time navigating the discipline and care of the children while trying to bond as a couple. It was a learning experience for both of them, and a challenging one at that. Fortunately, they have made it through and are still happily together. The children are grown, and while it has not been easy, Leah and Ethan are making it work as a couple and as a family.

The myth of the Brady Bunch type family is just that—a

myth. The idea that people can quickly and easily let go of their pasts is also a myth. Everyone carries forward *something* from his or her past relationship or marriage that will get triggered in the next one. Later in this book, we will explore what people can do to allow themselves to have the memories, but not necessarily the explosive or tearful reaction to them that they tend to project onto their partner in their next marriage.

I have covered in this chapter just a small list of some of the myths and challenges of marrying again. My intention in sharing these is to encourage you to recognize what may have caused the unrealistic expectations that have disappointed you or may cause an upcoming challenge. My wish for you, as a reader, is the opportunity to receive support by reading this book and doing the exercises in each chapter.

Chapter 2

UNDERSTANDING THE TEN PHASES OF RELATIONSHIPS

"Marriage is a book in which the first chapter is written in poetry and the remaining chapters in prose."

— Beverly Nichols

And you thought the flow of relationships was random, right? Yeah, I did too, a long time ago, but I realized at some point that a sequence and flow exist. I figured this out just in time for my second marriage. (Whew!) So now that we've explored a few myths and challenges of remarriage, let's look at the relationship journey that all marriages go through. Many relationships and even marriages completely crash and burn before they even make it through all of these phases, but whether the earlier phases lead to marriage or not, every relationship goes through many of these phases. Some of these phases happen just once, but some need to be repeated over and over to help the relationship or marriage thrive, and sadly, some get repeated over and over, causing perpetual conflict.

These phases begin as soon as two people meet, whether or not they have been divorced. You can look back on prior relationships you have had and even your prior marriage, and certainly your current one, to notice how these phases fit into your experiences. These phases can be graceful or challenging. If you look at them from a higher altitude, you can see the value in understanding them so you are prepared for them as they happen.

1) **The Courtship Phase:** Yes, this is the fun phase. You meet someone new, you feel an amazing attraction and some off the chart chemistry with this person, and you begin to date. Everything feels so fantastic! The romance is in full force! The clouds part, the flowers bloom, the birds sing, you forget your own name, and this haze of an ecstatic "buzz" is all around you. You may find you finish each other's sentences, and you feel like you are floating on some kind of cloud you've never been on before. Everyone is on his or her best behavior, trying to impress the other and prove his or her worth and sense of value. You may feel that this relationship is the best thing that has ever happened to you and that this person *must* be the one—must be your soul mate—because you are clear you both will live happily-ever-after. Many women (Sorry, ladies, I am picking on us for a moment) get really attached during this phase. It can be a hook

for women, especially if physical intimacy happens early on, but when it comes time to make the transition to the next phase, women begin to wonder what the hell just happened.

While the courtship phase is important for a couple to establish some initial chemistry bonding and it feels like a major "high," the challenge is that it is a one-time deal. That doesn't mean you will never feel "mushy and gooey" about your partner again after this phase; you will, but in a deeper and more unexpected way. But courtship is the "falling in love" phase, or at the very least, the initial connection and exploration of chemistry phase. Often for couples who aren't right for each other, but who have great chemistry, it ends up being the "lust and bust" phase. Unfortunately, some people think that because it feels so *amazing*, it is what a marriage will be like every day moving forward. Many engage in very specific expectations that this intense level of romance and buzz will continue forever. Guess what? A relationship and marriage is not intended to move forward in this intense courtship kind of way. Instead, a relationship is like a lifelong sprint and marriage is a marathon.

Most people want their relationships to go deeper, grow stronger, and be expansive. Therefore, view the courtship phase as an opportunity to "pre-qualify" a potential long-term partner, keeping in mind that in the haze of major physical and sexual chemistry, blazing red flags are commonly missed. It is a fun phase, no doubt, but rarely a time to make long-term decisions as to whether it will become a forever marriage. Those who do make a long-term decision during this phase, especially in a remarriage, will still have to go through another phase that may bring up some conflict.

2) **The Exclusivity Phase:** The courtship has been going well, so you both want to explore the relationship and you agree to exclusive dating to see what unfolds. Exclusive dating takes the courtship phase one step further. You know it's just the two of you exploring the relationship together, and neither of you are dating anyone else at this point, nor do you want to. It is a fun phase as well, and you are still experiencing an "Oh, my God" high and feeling the thrill of having a boyfriend or girlfriend and a future full of possibilities. This isn't necessarily a life commitment phase, although some will tell others they are in a committed relationship, but that really means they are exclusive and committed to the exploration. Enjoy this phase because it doesn't last long before phase three happens.

3) **The Integration Phase:** The integration phase and the next phase, intention, can sometimes be interchangeable, but generally, integration will come first. During the integration phase, the happy "high haze" starts to clear, giving you the opportunity to see the real person you have been in a relationship with or exclusively dating for the past few months. You will finally see things you didn't notice before or just waved away. You may see and notice things you don't necessarily like about this person who until now has been the "greatest person

ever" since you met. There will be more "differentiating," meaning stepping back in to your individual life. You now begin to focus back on career, remember you have friends, and engage in some power struggles or conflicts with this beloved person who once was just perfect. At this point, men tend to slow down on the wooing and courting, leaving women to wonder what the hell happened to make this perfect man more distant and slightly less attentive than before. This is the make it or break it phase. This is the time to qualify and evaluate because you are finally seeing the bigger picture of this exclusive relationship and the more authentic version of this person. Here is where the relationship may fall apart and end, or the couple understands that they can grow through their issues and each understand all facets of the other, loving and accepting each other for who they are and who they are not. This is truth time. This is the time to qualify someone to see whether he or she fits your ideal mate criteria and whether the two of you fit into an ideal relationship with marriage potential.

4) **The Intention Phase:** Congratulations. If you get to this phase, you have gotten through some integration and now feel like you want to set an intention. This is the phase filled with promise rings, engagements, and moving in together, all with the intention of moving into the ultimate commitment—marriage. It is still a time of evaluation. For those couples already engaged to be married, it is a time for planning the future, for focusing on the upcoming wedding, and for setting intentions for the marriage. For those living together, the intention

might be to "try it on" and "see if it fits." There is a steady climb to the commitment phase, and things can still be integrating as well. Couples can still be qualifying each other and evaluating. Merging together with the intention to commit fully can bring up some conflict as the couple begins to grow closer. Some couples get stuck in this phase, mixed with the previous one, and still land in constant conflict. I'll discuss the reason for that later in the book. This can be a game-ender phase as well if a couple can't figure out how to manage conflict; then one or both will just throw in the towel, say, "Peace out," and bolt.

5) **The Commitment Phase:** Ring those wedding bells and say your "I dos." This is the ultimate level of relationship commitment, and it feels like a boost of the amazing high felt during courtship (which is a beautiful thing). However, it is often followed by some level of grief. After all, you've been planning your wedding or commitment ceremony for a while. It doesn't matter if you have a big wedding, a commitment ceremony, or an elopement; something shifts, and it is hard to verbalize what it is. You just feel it. If you were previously married, you may understand what I am referring to. Something changes when people get married or have a ceremony of some kind, and that change can really bring people closer together in both a good way and in a way that causes them to start projecting their issues onto each other. It is a time of great joy, a bit of grief, and a lot of adjustment. It's said that the first year of marriage can be the most challenging. For many couples, that is

the case. You must adjust to being a married person, even if you've been married before, and joining together on all levels shifts the union in many ways and brings up expectations as well as old issues, patterns, and beliefs that may not have been previously communicated.

6) **The Alignment Phase:** So you have been married for a bit and have been going through some of the wobbly adjustments, the great highs, and the challenging lows of the early stages of marriage. Now you have worked out the kinks, understand the projections, have learned some communication and conflict resolution skills, and feel you are finally in alignment. Things are working well again, and you have gotten your rhythm down. It is a nice time for couples to feel they have moved past the adjustment and have figured out how to align in marriage. This is a pleasant feeling and a lovely time for couples.

7) **The Synergy Phase:** And it only gets better moving from alignment to synergy. Alignment is like finally reaching the next level of the mountain climb. Synergy is feeling like you have mastered the mountain and have reached a higher, more stable peak with an incredible view. You are in the zone with each other; you have great rituals, inside jokes, and a shared sense of humor that make you, as a couple, uniquely you. You have balanced your individual pursuits with your couples' time and "we" goals. You have got it figured out between the two of you, and you are really enjoying it. This is a beautiful time in your marriage, and it is what you have been striving for. The key is figuring out how to maintain it.

8) **The Mindfulness Phase:** Mindfulness is more than just a phase. It is a way of being that every couple needs to master. Mindfulness is like minding the store; you consistently tend to the marriage, caring for and nurturing it, to ensure you are still on track. A marriage needs constant time, love, and attention, so this phase must keep going in order for couples to stay on track.

9) **The Evolution Phase:** This phase is also ongoing. Evolution in a relationship is all about personal, spiritual growth, and deep transformation. A relationship or marriage will give you many opportunities to grow. The relationship or marriage will itself also naturally evolve over time, so both partners need to evolve personally and as a couple. If you are practicing relationship mindfulness, the next step in the evolution will become clear to you as opportunities for healing and growth arise.

10) **The Transition Phase:** This phase can be very challenging. It occurs when there is a lifestyle transition of some sort, such as the empty nest phase of a marriage with children, the beginning of parenthood, a move or relocation, or a change in career. It can also be a time when the relationship or marriage itself comes to a completion after careful consideration and accepting that it has sadly run its course. The hardest transition of all is when a spouse or partner dies. It is the most painful transition because it involves more grief than any other transitions that happen throughout the life of a relationship.

Can you recognize these phases in your current or past relationships? As someone in a marriage or in a pre-marital phase who is or is soon to be remarried, you have already gone through these phases. Perhaps in your first marriage, you never reached synergy, or you weren't being as mindful as possible. Regardless, you evolved as a person in that previous marriage so take that evolution phase with you into your next relationship. You have grown, and the version of you that you are now has the opportunity to understand these phases and apply some of them to this remarriage experience.

Exercise:

Where are we as a couple now? What phases have we gone through, and what is happening in our current phase?

____

____

____

____

____

____

What do we need to do to be consistently mindful?

____

____

____

____

____

____

____

Chapter 3

INGREDIENT 1—GETTING BACK IN THE GAME

"Every person has to love at least one bad partner in life to be truly thankful for the right one."

— Author Unknown

This chapter is for those of you who have gone through marriage already, been divorced or widowed, are single again, and are seeking to get back in the game because your heartfelt desire *is* to be married again and to the *right* person this time. You also want to make sure you get marriage right this time. However, if you are already remarried or planning your next wedding, read this chapter anyway because there may be some little golden nuggets of information for you, and certainly for any of your divorced friends who have been too nervous to get back in the game.

If you are still in that space of being divorced and seeking new partnership, you already had the "so-called" bad partner, right? And you have learned *a lot* from your first marriage, yes? Yep, I did, too. In fact, I think first marriages are incredible teachers—painful ones, yes—but mine left me with more wisdom and more clarity, and if it weren't for that experience, I wouldn't have been ready for the marriage I have now. You want things to be different the next time around, right? Of course you do. I did, too. So what is going to make it different?

The first key is to own your part in what happened in your previous marriage. Uh, no one wants to do that. Isn't it easier to focus on what your previous spouse did wrong? Sure it is, but will that help you have a successful marriage moving forward? Nope.

In this chapter, we will be talking about taking ownership in your life and marriage, and looking at the part you played in your previous marriage that resulted in divorce. Yes, no matter what happens, we all play a part in how love shows up for us. The intention is to learn from that, like you would learn from a class, and have a better marriage ahead. So as you look back and reflect, can you see your part?

Sometimes, your part may be how you saw yourself, and what you believed about yourself, about marriage, and about your expectations. Perhaps you lacked self-esteem in a deep way and learned how *not* to love yourself. Perhaps you chose to marry before you were clear about what you were really looking for, or with not knowing the skills it takes to be in a successful marriage; you may have thought a spouse would complete you, prove your worth, and provide you with so many other critical but missing pieces. Does that belief make you a bad or stupid person? Of course not! Were we taught about relationships or marriage in school? No, we weren't. Our religions and spiritual communities may teach us certain things about marriage that align with their doctrines, but the truth is we grow up not getting much relationship education, so we enter into relationships and marriage without a manual and we wing it. We don't always know how to "pre-qualify" or evaluate whether someone is a good match for us, and we normally get caught up in certain aspects that don't encompass the totality of how we need to evaluate someone to see whether there is a true match.

Does that make you a horrible human being? Of course not. When I was divorced and ready to get back in the game, I still wasn't sure what I was doing for a while. I didn't know how to be in a successful marriage. I didn't even know how to prepare myself for one, so how could I have a successful one? I had a lot to learn, and there was plenty I didn't know that I didn't know.

The first thing I needed to learn was to look at my role in what had made my first marriage experience challenging. That wasn't easy because my first husband's behavior made it easy for me to blame him. However, I took this reflection a step further by going back to review my relationships prior to my first marriage.

In this book's introduction, I shared that I had noticed some similar patterns in most of my previous relationships. So I had to ask myself who the common denominator was and work with the fact that it was me.

Getting back in the game meant I had to know my part, my patterns, my relationship with myself, as well as my own feelings of self-worth. I was working on it, but I was still fuzzy about it as I went into the next relationship and noticed that, this time, I had met a kind person who was a great guy, but who didn't quite fit what I was looking for.

My past pattern was to convince a man that I was the "one" rather than to qualify a man to see whether he was the one for me. Another pattern was to "pretzel" myself into who I thought this man wanted so he would choose me. The truth is that I hung on to relationships that really didn't work for me, for many reasons. Sometimes being an empath meant that I could feel the suffering of others and thought I could rescue someone from his pain. Other patterns were about convincing someone to pick me, love me, choose me and to contort or pretzel myself into becoming whom they wanted me to be so I would be chosen. and in this situation with this kind guy, I didn't really want to hear what he was trying to tell me or face the truth I knew deep inside. I didn't want to face the truth that we just weren't the right match for each other.

Beginning with the integration phase of our relationship, he told me he thought I was the greatest gal he had ever known, but he didn't feel he was in love with me, nor did he think he ever would be. I was stunned to hear this because his actions suggested otherwise. Being the nice guy he was, and being the "convincer" I was, we decided to continue to explore our relationship. Time passed, and he told me again that while he had love for me and thought I was the greatest gal ever, he wasn't clear that he was in love with me. Rinse, repeat....

Did I get the message that time? Nope.

Instead, I attended a workshop about "creating your future." In the workshop, I determined that my one-year goal was to get remarried. As instructed, I worked backwards, starting from my end point (being remarried) and put together a timeline with events leading up to that end point, such as buying a wedding dress, spending time with my bridesmaids, picking out our flowers and cake, etc. I decided that four days before the weekend workshop graduation was when I would become engaged. Then I could announce my engagement to our class. Yup, I was a convincer at that time and was very intentional.

When I went home and shared this with my then nice guy boyfriend, he couldn't stop laughing. We talked for hours about it, and his truth was that he wasn't ready. He had never been married, was about seven years younger than me, and just had other goals he wanted to accomplish prior to being married. Plus there was the lack of clarity about whether or not he was in love with me. While I understood that, I stuck to my intention and carried on with my action steps for the class anyway.

My next step was to go to a jewelry store and choose an engagement-wedding ring set. I randomly picked a store and chose a set I liked. Time was running out for me to be engaged before the course "graduation," so I decided I had to let go of the idea that I would be able to share the amazing news with my class that I was so powerful that I actually got engaged.

The next evening, my then nice boyfriend came over to me on

our couch and shockingly proposed. It turns out he had gone into the same jewelry store I had, not knowing I had even been there, and picked out a smaller version of the ring I had chosen. For some reason, the salesperson, who remembered me, realized this was my prospective fiancé, so he showed him the rings I had liked.

Imagine the shock on my face when my "nice but not that into me" boyfriend became my fiancé. I saw it as a sign that this relationship was going to work out.
Of course, the following night at the course graduation, I excitedly shared the powerful story of my engagement with everyone. I got a huge standing ovation filled with thunderous applause, and I felt on top of the world.

A few months later, my now fiancé questioned things again. He repeated that he wasn't sure he was in love with me or that I was "the one," but he still felt I was the greatest gal ever. I kept convincing him that we were the right fit for one another, even though I wasn't even sure I believed it myself. He said he wanted to get a house because it was one of his important goals, so we spent several months house hunting, found a home, bought it, and moved in. A week later, I woke up, and it hit me like a ton of bricks: I was with the wrong guy! Yikes!

I realized now that I had spent so much time trying to convince him to love me and that I was the one for him that I hadn't qualified him to see whether he was the one for me. I had recently started grad school, and one of our assignments was to explore visualizing our future. As I created my vision for a relationship, and was completely honest with myself, I had the ultimate clarity that I wasn't with the right person, as nice as he was. That clarity was my final answer to whether or not we would marry.

I contemplated what to do next, considering that we had just bought and moved into a house. Through my grad school program in psychology, I was able to explore my own personal issues and patterns very quickly, and I knew what I had done. That was an "Oh, shit" moment for me, for sure, but it was also a powerful awakening about my own part in my first marriage and in this current relationship. The greatest revelation was *why* I was trying to convince men to love me. I was so busy trying to convince a man of my worth, of how good enough I was, of how pretty enough I was, and how loving and giving I was, that I had forgotten to focus on whether or not the man was the best fit for *me*. That important piece of awareness ultimately changed my love life and my life overall forever.

Once I came to this realization and explained it to my fiancé, who was "relieved," we spent a few months figuring out how to break up logistically and amicably. During the process, I also realized I was developing feelings for my male grad school study buddy. Uh oh! I had no idea what this guy thought about me beyond being a great friend, and since my "convincing" days were now over, I did nothing except be his friend.

Then I did something I generally do not recommend. One night, my grad school "friend" sent me a love letter, out of the blue. I was stunned since I had no idea he had feelings for me in that way. I was also giddy as hell, but I had to think about whether I needed some time between relationships. So I discussed it with my "friend" and we decided to remain just friends. But I just had a deep intuitive sense that this was the right guy for me. I didn't have to convince him of anything, and since he was my friend and I had already gotten to know him, I knew he was already "qualified." Two months after the initial love letter, in May 2001, we decided to elope. We both just knew.

Now, again, I don't recommend going from one relationship to the next like that, but that's how things unfolded. I do feel I stayed with my former fiancé much longer than I should have. If I had listened to him and listened to myself and not been hell bent on convincing him to love me, I would have ended things much sooner and just been friends.

For many people, getting back in the game can be a slower process of dating than it was for me. Yes, it can be a home run on the first step up at bat, but it can also be a series of strikeouts before that home run is hit.

Since getting back in the game is important, let's look at what it consists of. Here are some key points to understand before you take the step of dating again:

1) It really isn't a game—I am just using that as a metaphor.

2) Know the part you played in the previous marriage and the patterns you have had in previous relationships that didn't work out and own them.

3) Do your healing and clearing work for past issues. These

techniques will be shared later in this book.

4) Know who you are and what you really are looking for in a relationship or marriage. These steps will also be shared later.

5) Learn to qualify rather than convince. You never need to try to convince someone to love you, or pretzel yourself to be whom you think this person wants you to be, and if you do, you may be overstaying your welcome and not seeing something else wonderful that may be right in front of you.

6) Learn that dating is a process of exploration, qualification, and deepening your intuition about yourself, valuing yourself, and learning about the people you are dating.

7) Know your personal guidelines for the dating process. Clarify those boundaries and stick to them.

8) Know that some relationships move fast and some don't, but get to the Integration Phase before you make *any* decisions so you can see how authentic the person is whom you are with and also be the most authentic version of yourself.

9) Learn to trust your own inner wisdom, love yourself, and honor your own criteria, guidelines, and boundaries.

10) Take the time you need. There is no rush to be married again. Being single again is not a shameful scarlet letter; it's just being single again. There is no need to make it mean that there is something wrong with you.

These are some tips for getting back in the game if you want to remarry. There are many other aspects, which are personal to each of you reading this book, and of course, hiring a coach like me to take you through the process is a great commitment to yourself and your heartfelt dream of finding your true soul mate.

If you are not remarried but wish to be, are you ready to get back in the game?

Exercise:

1) In my previous marriage I can now see that my part was:

____

____

____

____

____

____

____

2) In my relationships prior to my past marriage, I can now see that I had a tendency to and a pattern of:

____

____

____

____

____

____

____

3) If I look at the ten steps to getting back in the game described above, I know I need to work on:

____

____

____

____

____

____

____

____

4) The issues that I feel are getting in my way now are:

____

____

____

____

____

____

____

____

5) What I need to do to have a better relationship with myself, experience more love for myself, and value myself more are:

____

____

____

____

____

____

____

____

6) Some action steps I can take to course correct or move myself closer to my dream of being remarried are:

____

____

____

____

____

____

____

____

Chapter 4

INGREDIENT 2— BEING IN THE KNOW (INCREASING AWARENESS)

"One of the most amazing gifts in life is to find someone who knows all your flaws, differences, and mistakes, yet still loves everything about you."

— Author Unknown

In the last chapter, we looked at getting back in the game to seek love and marriage again, following some time after a divorce. In this chapter, we will look at an important aspect of remarriage or any marriage, really. Part of the integration phase I spoke about earlier is seeing the *reality* of the person you were thinking was so perfect. Evaluating that person's level of clarity and awareness, as well as your own will, allow both of you to be on the same page about your marriage moving forward. No one wants to be with a partner who is so clueless that the person will drive him- or herself "into a ditch," has no idea what you are all about, or isn't even clear about his or her own inner workings. If you can't seem to know what your partner might need at the grocery store when you are shopping for him or her, chances are, that is the tip of the iceberg for needing to be "in the know" about yourself and about your partner.

Being married before may have baffled you and your previous partner because you didn't have the depth of information you needed to succeed. I remember my level of clarity in my first marriage—I wanted someone who was kind, funny, and nice to me, with beautiful eyes and a cute butt. Sure there was more on my list than that, but not much. I was embarrassingly clueless about what I wanted and what marriage was all about. Many couples who are married at a younger age tend to avoid learning what is essential to them prior to getting married, so they are shocked when there is a lot of conflict, or they have "Oh, shit" moments when they come to a higher level of awareness and realize that marriage is not the fairy tale they imagined it would be.

One of the things that baffled me the most about my first marriage was how clueless my former husband seemed about himself, his life, and me. I admit that yes, I, too, was also pretty clueless. Compared to him, I did have a higher level of awareness about what was really going on, but I didn't hold to my then small list of what I call core values, core essentials, must haves, and deal breakers. The red flags were a-blazin' during our dating process (if you want to call it that—we didn't really date formally; we just hung out), but I pretended those red flags didn't exist. I was a bit baffled and frustrated, but I was one of those gals who just thought this man would change. My mistake was not taking action because, deep down, I knew those red flags were actually my deal breakers. Instead, I waited, hoped, and prayed that he and the relationship-turned-marriage would magically transform. What I became aware of, as I evolved, was more information about myself and my own values. I became clearer about what I wanted out of life, what I wanted out of marriage, and what I wanted in a partner, and it was crystal clear that I didn't have any of what I wanted with him. A different man was a better fit for me, and a different woman was a better fit for him.

Awareness is the first tool to have in your toolbox because awakening to the truth of yourself, your beliefs, your expectations, your patterns, your issues, your wounds of the past, your stories, your core values, your core essential needs, your must haves, and your deal breakers will all allow you to see the marriage and yourself from a higher altitude and notice a lot more of the truth about it. Then you can compare it to what you truly are looking for. Looking back on your first marriage, you may now see these things clearly. They are great lessons to have learned, and even if you are now knee-deep in your current marriage and things aren't going well again, you can both gain clarity about your own levels of awareness.

In many marriages, someone gets "triggered" or becomes upset about something. A trigger brings up a thought or emotion based on something that someone said or did. It brings up old emotions, and what I call "stories" or limiting beliefs, creating a not-so-happy reaction inside. Being aware of what is a trigger for you is key. The source of that trigger isn't going to heal if you make it about the other person and blame him or her. Most people will not be aware that they said or did something that pushed a trigger button in you. (If they are aware, that's a different story!) Be aware of your triggers, and if necessary, share them with your partner to avoid conflict and create understanding between the two of you. Being aware of that bigger picture and what makes you and your partner tick inside and out can make or break a marriage.

A couple I worked with came to me with a conflict. It was her first marriage and his second. She had not married until well into her forties and had high expectations for her husband and the level of awareness he should have. He had been married previously, but he wasn't as clear about his own patterns, issues, stories, and beliefs. She was triggered a lot by his lack of clarity, and she constantly got on his case about not helping out around the house, not being more ambitious about his career, not being motivated to make more money, and basically, not living life the way she expected him to live it.

While she had a lot of life experience, she didn't have a lot of relationship experience, and her high expectations started to eat away at her husband's self-esteem until he started to shut down. He had followed this same pattern in his family of origin and in his first marriage. By working with both of them, I was able to help them reach a level of higher awareness about many parts of their marriage and aspects of themselves, and they were then able to recognize their own part in why they had a lot of conflict. They were also then able to recognize their partner's needs, old wounds, and expectations. Had they not raised their depth of awareness and learned to notice, ask questions, and tune into themselves and each other while being fully present to themselves, the marriage may not have survived. There is no need for someone not to have authentic expectations, but if those expectations are not compatible with a partner's behavior and expectations, it can be quite challenging. We will address this topic in more detail in our next chapter.

Exercise:

Take a look at your marriage.

What are you aware of about the "state of your union"?

____

____

____

____

____

How can you deepen your own level of awareness about yourself and your partner? How can you become even more aware of your own process and that of your partner?

____

____

____

____

____

Chapter 5

INGREDIENT 3—SEEING CLEARLY NOW

"No partner in a love relationship should feel like they have to give up an essential part of themselves to make it viable."

— *May Sarton*

Does our level of awareness increase as we get older and move on to new relationships? Hopefully, it does! As I mentioned in the last chapter, we tend to be somewhat clueless as younger people in first marriages, but hopefully, we see life and love more clearly when we marry again. Does awareness always unfold that way? Nope. So this chapter offers a way to be more in tune so you can be clear that this is the right person for you and that you will be entering the type of marriage you really want to have.

If you are already remarried, go through this chapter and do the exercises. Uncover the critical pieces that may need some improvement or even may be missing. You can fret about these pieces if you choose, but there are better ways to bring things back together in a more aligned and synergistic way. If you gather this information and realize that you've "stepped in it again" to the degree that you really want an escape hatch, you can certainly find a dignified way to exit. It is tough when you gain higher clarity and have an "Oops, I did it again" moment where you become aware that you chose a person who isn't really the best fit to be your spouse. Hopefully, that is not the case, but if you do find some inconsistencies, get some support, such as a pretty knowledgeable relationship coach (wink, wink).

So let's look at what I hope everyone explores prior to meeting at the altar, but if not, and you have that "Oh shit" moment, we can look at your options. In the rest of this chapter, we'll look at knowing your core values, core essential needs, and your must haves and deal breakers. Let's begin.

Core Values

You might think you already know your core values, but you will be surprised by the way I'm going to have you look at them. Core values can be qualities such as compassion or honesty, but they can also be categories such as home, money, or career. Here's a process for determining them:

1) Start by making a list of as many core values as you can think of for life in general. Are they qualities such as compassion, love, or things like home, family, career, etc.?

2) Then make a list of your marriage core values. Again, they can be qualities you want in partnership or things you want in partnership. You can make this list by yourself and share it with your partner, or you can do it with your partner.

3) Give each core value a definition because two people can say the same word but have two different definitions for it, which could cause an "Oh, shit" moment (especially if the value is "monogamy").

4) Now, here is the kicker: Look at your lists but make another one. What goes on this list? What you are actually focusing on in your life. Notice where you really spend your time and energy. This is the list that will really tell you what you value. Why? Because this is the truth of what you are spending time doing; therefore, these are your priorities and the things you value. Yes, it is accurate to think that there are some "have-to" items on this list, but if you look at why you are doing them, you will see where the core value is.

____
____
____
____
____
____
____

5) Create a list like this for your marriage as well. As a couple, what are you spending your time and energy doing? Where is your focus as a couple?

____
____
____
____
____
____
____

6) Prioritize the lists and narrow them down to your Top Ten Core Values with definitions.

1. ______________________________

2. ______________________________

3. ______________________________

4. ______________________________

5. ______________________________

6. ______________________________

7. ______________________________

8. ______________________________

9. ______________________________

10. ______________________________

Core Essential Needs

Core essential needs can be emotional needs such as affection, housekeeping needs such as "Get your crap off the floor because I like things clean," or even things you won't tolerate such as to have your partner stop smoking. This list of needs includes items that would annoy you if not met, but would not end the marriage. Conflict can erupt, but this level of conflict can be resolved with the right tools. (And, of course, I will present some good ones in a future chapter.)

1) Brainstorm your practical and emotional core essential needs.

____
____
____
____
____
____
____
____
____
____
____
____
____

2) Narrow down your list to your Top Five. Define them and share them with your partner

   1. ____
   2. ____
   3. ____
   4. ____
   5. ____

Finally, we have the most challenging list of all:

Must Haves/Deal Breakers

This is the "big kahuna" list because whatever you write is something you must have in a relationship or marriage. You can't move forward without it because the absence of it is a deal breaker. If there is even one deal breaker in the marriage, it can end the marriage.

An example would be a couple I worked with who were what I call a "combo couple." A combo couple is a partnership in which one person has been married before and the other has never been married. (More on that later.) Let me give you a story as an example.

Ashley and Darrin got married with the agreement that they would have a baby. Darrin already had two teenagers from a previous marriage, so it was decided that when those kids were both in college, he and Ashley would have a baby of their own.

So, time went by and Darrin's youngest finally went off to college. Ashley was very ready to start trying for a baby, but by then, Darrin had reflected more and ended up changing his mind. Yeah, I know! He felt he had raised kids and didn't want to do it again. A baby was a must have/deal breaker for Ashley. She was so upset and so in shock reflecting on what to do that she ended up having an affair. Cheating, of course, was a deal breaker for Darrin. So, two deal breakers landed this marriage in divorce.

Divorce often requires just one deal breaker so when making your must have and deal breaker lists below, take your time and be completely honest with yourself. This is a great start, and I encourage you to have a notebook for your full lists.

1) **My Must Haves:**

____

____

____

____

____

2) **My Deal Breakers:**

____

____

____

____

____

3) **Definitions of Must Haves and Deal Breakers:**

____

____

____

____

____

4) **Discuss and share with your partner**

If you find there is a must have that is not getting met and that has caused conflict or a deal breaker that you just haven't addressed, now is the time to do so. I know discussing deal breakers can be scary because no one wants to be in a position to consider another divorce, so I again recommend working with a relationship and marriage coach (like me) or some kind of marriage expert to help you through this process. There will be decisions to make if deal breakers come up or even if there are conflicts in the core essential needs area, and a coach can help you make those decisions impartially and in the most fair way to both of you.

My wish is that your list will be honored in your marriage because if you were married before, likely something was a deal breaker or a must have was missing. Having that happen again would be heartbreaking.

Understanding your must haves and deal breakers is a critical piece of remarrying right. The last thing you want is to find out your second or third marriage isn't what you thought it was, but as scary as it is to look at this area, it must be examined in order to move forward into a happy marriage.

Make sure these lists are in alignment, are authentic to you, and are not just items that will please your partner or prevent you from having to have tough conversations. Make sure you honor yourself and your partner. You may find that some of your core values are also must haves or deal breakers, and that is okay.

My husband Rick and I did this exercise before and during our marriage, and fortunately, all came out well. (Yeah, we pretty much knew it would.) Doing it before we got married was very helpful. Doing a check-in years later was a good exercise, and continuing to do periodic check-ins helps our marriage stay really healthy. We have never had a lot of major conflict, so we were pretty sure all would be fine. We talk to each other in depth quite a bit, so we keep up with any issues that may come up and resolve them as quickly, yet as thoroughly and as consciously, as possible. I highly recommend not sweeping anything under the rug just to stay in your marriage. Be authentic and honest with one another. While ending a marriage is gut-wrenching and nowhere near ideal, getting another divorce is better than staying in a painful marriage that doesn't work.

I have worked with too many couples who didn't clarify these important items, and consequently, things didn't end well once they were able to sort out why their marriage wasn't working.

Chapter 6

INGREDIENT 4—TALKING POINTS: AVOIDING COMMUNICATION PITFALLS

"A person isn't who they are during the last conversation you had with them. They're who they've been throughout the entire relationship."

— Rainer Maria Rilke

Haven't we all heard the cliché statement "Communication is the key to a successful marriage"? Cliché or not, communication is a very critical part of marriage, perhaps one of the most important ingredients for a successful one. In the last chapter, I spoke about how important it is to know yourself, your core values, essential needs, must haves, and deal breakers. Good, effective communication usually finds itself on one of those lists, so let's talk about it, shall we?

If two people in a marriage can't consciously speak to each other or really hear each other well, then "Houston, we have a problem." I can't stress enough how critical conscious and effective communication is. If you're divorced, then it is likely that some of the communication pitfalls I'm about to share were common. I will break these pitfalls down for you into categories of language that does not work, language that does work, tone that inflames the situation, the importance of non-verbal communication, and what I call "the lost habit of positive communication." Now that you are remarrying right or remarried and want to get it right, it is important to understand all of the pitfalls, to practice course correcting them, and to make more effective communication choices (which we'll talk about in the next chapter).

Let's start with some of the most common pitfalls that most couples fall into and why. Here's my Top Ten Communication Pitfalls list that we'll explore in detail for the rest of this chapter:

1. The Blame Game
2. Always & Never
3. Right & Wrong
4. Listening (but not really)
5. Avoidance
6. Yelling
7. Sarcasm

8. Interrupting
9. Playing the Victim
10. Name Calling

The Blame Game

First, we have the "Blame Game." What is the blame game? Basically, any sentence that starts with the word "you" that isn't a compliment or a neutral statement is intended to blame or complain. Here are some examples (Insert some snarky tone):

- "You did _______."
- "You made me feel like________."
- "You didn't do___________."
- "You said__________."
- "You didn't say_____________."

I could go on with examples, but I imagine you get the point. What is really happening inside of the person who uses this type of language and directs it toward his or her loved one? What is it really about for the blamer? Likely, the person directing the blame is being triggered by an old issue, pattern, or belief, and it has brought forward strong, negative thoughts (stories and beliefs) and negative, reactive emotions. The person's partner may have said or done something that accidentally (or, sadly, sometimes intentionally) pushed that trigger button, and it brought up something that made the person want to blame his or her partner for his or her own feelings. What is the other person thinking in that moment? He or she is getting triggered with some kind of negative emotional reaction and formulating a defensive comeback blame statement. Most people who feel they are being blamed, scolded, or attacked in some way aren't going to respond so kindly or even hear what their partner is saying once they feel triggered and defensive. This is pretty much guaranteed to start some kind of conflict. Few people are going to sit back, listen to that, and say: "Sure, honey, you are right; I totally suck." We will get into several discussions later about taking personal ownership for our own thoughts, feelings, interpretations, and actions, but this way of communicating actually demonstrates *not* taking that ownership, not taking personal responsibility, and making it about the partner rather than owning our part. Most people in a second or third marriage have already had the experience of being and feeling blamed. It hurts, it sucks, and it doesn't create a great flow of conscious communication.

Note to all: One of the statements I hear all of the time is "He/she made me feel________ or makes me feel like ______________." Truth? No one *makes* you feel anything. You know those statements: "You made me angry. You made me feel bad. Why aren't you making me happy?" Someone says something and you react how you do. It's not that the person *made* you feel anything. You already had those feelings inside of you, and your partner's words and/or tone just triggered them. So for anyone who uses this type of language to communicate and wishes to see his or her partner feel bad, just know it is *not* going to elicit the response you want. From there, it just ignites conflict. (We will discuss better ways to manage conflict shortly.)

Here is another blame game conversation example with my personal commentary in parentheses:

Marge: Steve, you made me feel like crap when you didn't get me flowers on Valentine's Day.

(Marge, honey, you already felt like crap; in fact, you felt like that before Steve came along.)

Steve: What the hell? I got you a diamond necklace. Isn't that good enough for you?

Marge: Okay, yeah, it was a nice necklace, but you should have gotten me flowers, too. It's Valentine's Day, for goodness sake. Nellie next door got flowers and a new car.

(Oh, Marge, greed is not good….)

Steve: Fine. Next year, I won't get you anything since you don't appreciate me.

(Steve, you probably didn't feel appreciated prior to this conversation.)

There's no winner in this conversation. Marge is blaming Steve, comparing her gifts to someone else's, not appreciating her husband, and holding him responsible for the fact that she feels bad. That is a long conflict that will continue on for a while, filled with resentment and old wounds that have nothing to do with the other person or the actual gifting.

Here's another blame game example with my commentary:

Steve: Marge, you didn't do the dishes. I work all day long and I come home to no clean plates or dinner, and now I have to wash a plate in order to eat something?

(Seriously, Steve? Washing a plate takes two minutes. Chill, dude, and wash a dish.)

Marge: Well, I work all day, too, Steve, and you are being ridiculous. You are acting like a child wanting Mommy to do everything for you. I don't have a clean plate either, and no, dinner isn't made yet. Get over yourself.

Steve: You are so inept, Marge. All I ask is that I come home to some food and a plate to eat it on; is that too much to ask?

(Steve, she is going to take points off for that one.)

Marge: You're not twelve, Steve, and again, you know I

work, too, so you need to get over it and be patient. I'm not your cook or your maid.

(This is not going well, guys.)

Steve: Well, now I'm hungry, have to wait, and it's your fault.

Marge: Well, why don't you actually cook something for once?

(Yikes!)

You can see here how the conflict brews, yet there is no real resolution in sight, just back and forth defensiveness, upset emotions, and blame. That's not a productive, kind, or conscious conversation, and it is communication that is completely ineffective. Note that there is some name calling here as well. The Blame Game tends to bring that out in people. In our next chapter, we will look at better ways to communicate than doing so through blame.

Always & Never

Next, we have the delightful words *always* and *never*.

What literally astounds me about the use of these words (and yes, I've fallen into this pit as well) is that no one is really keeping an Excel spreadsheet to document whether something always or never happens. Using these words is just a way of being dramatic and extreme in order to make a point. One thing I will say is that those words aren't received well by anyone because everyone knows damn well that always or never isn't the case. So what happens when they are used? People are getting defensive and argumentative. They tune out the deeper issue of the conversation because they are so focused on being dramatic with the use of *always* or *never*.

Here's an example of an *always* and *never* conversation with my commentary:

Beverly: Biff, you were supposed to take the car to be washed. You never do the things I ask you to do, and you always make some kind of excuse about it.

(Really, Bev, never?)

Biff: What do you mean I never do anything you ask? I just mowed the lawn when you asked me to yesterday. I didn't take the car in because I worked later than expected and had planned on doing it the first opportunity I had.

Beverly: See, you always make an excuse.

Biff: Always? Do you keep documentation on that, Bev? Do you honestly think I never do anything around here and always make excuses? If you do, you haven't been in this marriage for the last twenty-two years; either that or you're just an idiot who doesn't appreciate what I do and who doesn't pay attention. You, know,

Bev, you never appreciate what I do or the fact that I work to provide for this family.

(Uh oh, Biff; points off for name calling.)

Beverly: See, there you go, getting mean again. You're always mean to me when I call you out because you neglected to do something I asked you to do. You never admit to it.

Biff: You know what, Bev? I'm going to go upstairs because I can't even have a civilized conversation with you. My first wife at least acknowledged when I did my best to do something.

(Low blow, Biff.)

Whoa, that last part had to sting. Ouch! You see why *always* and *never* are not the best choice of words to use. First of all, they are likely not even true. Second of all, no one is keeping the spreadsheet to document any of this. If someone is, he or she is more committed to making his or her partner look wrong than to having a successful marriage.

What might work better? We will find out in our next chapter.

Right & Wrong

Avoiding the words *right* and *wrong* is a tough one

because we all have egos that want to be right and cannot stand being wrong or feeling that they are being made to look wrong.

Once when I worked with a couple who had this issue, the husband said how much he just wanted to "win" and that was why he was arguing to be right. I will share with all of you that being right wins no prize in any marriage. There is no winner here. No one wants to feel *wrong* because wrong has a connotation with *bad*. Being right may have the illusion of feeling superior, but it doesn't make anyone superior. Neither of these terms inspires good communication. In fact, the Right and Wrong Game will lead to the Persistent Conflict and Resentment Game. People will even go so far as to exaggerate facts just to try to prove they are right and the other person is wrong. The ego is very strong in its wanting to be right.

Here's an example of a conversation using *right* and *wrong* with my commentary:

Sally was going to meet up with her sister and her sister's boyfriend for lunch. She didn't really like her sister's boyfriend too much, but she wanted to support her sister and do her best to get to know the guy more. Sally's husband, Vince, didn't see the point. His view was that if you don't like the guy, why even go? This was their exchange.

Vince: Sally, I don't get why you are going to lunch

with Christine and that guy Phil. We don't like Phil, and I don't want you to go. I don't think you should go. Why would anyone go to spend time with someone she doesn't like?

(That's your opinion, Vince.)

Sally: What do you mean, you don't want me to go? I want to support my sister. Maybe there is something about Phil that will be better than what we have seen.

(Good, Sally; be hopeful.)

Vince: You just don't bother going to these things when you don't like someone. That's just how it's done.

(According to whom, Vince? I don't recall a committee on this.)

Sally: I don't get what you mean when you say, "You just don't bother going."

Vince: I'm telling you, I'm right about this. You just don't go and you just don't support Christine if you don't like this guy so she can see that you don't support their relationship.

(Oh, Vince, being right has no winner.)

Sally: Seriously? I feel I want to support my sister.

That's what I think is right. What makes you think you know what is right?

(Good question, Sally.)

Vince: You're just wrong about this, and I don't understand why you are doing this. This guy is a loser. I'm totally right about this. I know it. Now you're wasting your time when *we* could have gone somewhere.

Sally: Wait a minute here; how is this *wrong*? I am really upset you are even saying this, and I don't have any idea what that's about.

Vince: It's wrong because you just don't do that.

(Okay, Vince, time to let go of that.)

Sally: Well, *thanks* (sarcasm) for your support. I'm sure Christine will really *appreciate* you (more sarcasm). I am going.

(Stand your ground, girl!)

Vince: I'm trying to support you and prevent you from having a lousy time.

Sally: How do you know I am going to have a lousy time?

Vince: Because I just know. The dude is a loser, and you're just going to be miserable.

(Are you psychic, Vince?)

Sally: You don't know that. I may actually enjoy myself.

Vince: No, you won't. I'm telling you.

Sally: Vince, stop trying to act like you're right. You have no idea what kind of time I'm going to have. That's it; I'm done talking to you about it.

Yeah, time out here….

So imagine this couple talking over each other in a yelling tone as well. This conversation just went nowhere positive. Vince seemed to have a "policy" of some sort that he thought was right, but Sally wasn't going for it.

As it turns out, Sally had a nice time, and even though Christine and Phil eventually broke up, that lunch was a pleasant experience for Sally. Sally shared this with Vince and requested that he not decide what is right for her in the future and respect her choices.

Listening (but not really)

This is a tricky one. Listening and being heard is a big need for people, especially women. There are moments when partners actually pretend to listen to each other. Imagine that! Sometimes, a person is really not up for a deep conversation, a long conversation. Sometimes, the brain's biology can interfere with listening, and sometimes, a person is just not interested in what a partner has to say, which, in my view, is pretty sad.

It is accurate to say that women speak more than men. According to the University of Maryland's College of Medicine, women use an average of 20,000 words a day, while men use an average of 7,000. Of course, that is an average, and some men can talk up a storm while some women don't, but for most couples, biology can be an issue that ends up being taken personally. In the world of listening, the right and left hemispheres of a man's brain do not connect like those of a woman. For that reason, women have a larger capacity for listening in one sitting, whereas men have to stop after a while because their brain capacity for listening shuts down and needs a rest. It's like women just get more miles to the gallon when it comes to speaking and listening than men do. Sadly, most people don't know these facts, so women tend to take it personally when they see that their male counterpart isn't listening or isn't hearing what they are saying. Men don't always know the best way to explain what is happening, so it all becomes one big, ugly conflict.

I've seen it and heard it with my own husband (not the conflict part, but the brain shutting off part). After I have been talking for a while (which happens quite often), I see his eyes start to gloss over, his head start to droop a little, and I hear, "Yeah, uh huh" before I even finish a sentence. Those are my signs that his brain is fried from conversation and it's time for him to rest it. Now, do I get angry about it? Not anymore because I understand what is happening. So I ask him if his brain is saturated and he needs a rest. He usually nods, takes a nap or rests, and then we can come back to the conversation later on. For me, is it a bummer? Sure, but I have other things to do and girlfriends whom I can call if I need to continue sharing.

However, most people don't understand the brain biology aspect, so women take it personally when men don't listen (or sometimes, vice versa), and it leads to conflict. In fact, men not listening is the number one complaint I get from women. Usually in first marriages, people are not looking to understand this type of information or to delve into a deep understanding about why certain things happen; they are just in the marriage experience and want what they want. Moving into remarriage, we tend to be more curious about why things are happening as they do and whether there is a solution for it.

Yes, there is a solution, which I will share in our next chapter.

While I have worked with several couples experiencing the listening issue, I worked with one couple in particular—I will call them Victoria and Billy (Yes, I'm a *The Young and the Restless* fan). Victoria liked to greet Billy at the door when he came home from work. She worked from home as a writer, and she was filled with so many things she wanted to share with Billy when he walked in the door.

Billy pretended to listen, but in truth, he was saturated from all of the words that had transpired from his workday, so he needed some down time before having a conversation with Victoria. But he didn't know how to say this to her; he loved her dearly and didn't want her feelings to be hurt. Meanwhile, Victoria sensed an absence in his energy, but her feelings were hurt anyway, thinking he didn't really care about what she had to say. So they got into a conflict about it. She asked whether he even cared about listening to her or sharing with her. He told her, "Of course I do, but I just can't do it the minute I walk in the door." She didn't understand this, so the conflict kept cycling.

Once I began working with them and explained about the brain biology, it helped them create their own solution, their own process, and all was well once again.

Avoidance

Often, one partner wants to discuss an issue while the other would prefer not to and avoids it like the plague. This person may become silent, may leave the room, may change the subject, and may even start pouting. Such avoidance demonstrates a lot of fears about communicating authentically, and perhaps also, the person's fear of being made to look wrong. It can be part of the brain biology as well, and likely in a partnership, there is one who tends to avoid while the other tends to be more anxious to have the conversation and pushes to have it until that person feels safe. This is an opportunity to face something by making time to discuss the issue and coming at it with an intention to resolve it rather than argue about it. Avoidance only leads to anger, resentment, and a lack of resolution.

Yelling

I'm not sure I even need to explain why yelling isn't a banner idea. It is clear that people get angry, but there is no situation where yelling at each other will truly resolve anything. If you feel like a volcano ready to erupt, take a time-out; tell your partner you are angry and need some time to sort through your feelings, and you will come back to the conversation later; then go process how you are feeling and why.

Sarcasm
I think we know how ineffective sarcasm is. No one wants to be on the receiving end of an intentionally sarcastic comment that was meant to sting. Ouch!

Interrupting
How can anyone hear anything? It is like a news show with political pundits talking over each other, each trying to make his or her point. Being so busy trying to get your words in while your partner is trying to do the same just results in no one being heard. When I work with clients who start interrupting each other and I'm

working by phone or Skype, they know ahead of time that I will push the mute button or call a time-out. I have a specific way I work with interrupting, and I teach couples how to manage that tendency.

Playing the Victim

Crying "Poor me" won't get the empathy you are hoping for. It just doesn't work. It's one thing to feel authentically sad about what your partner has said or done; it's another to exaggerate it to get some sympathy. Playing the "victim" role won't help the marriage progress. Regardless of how you feel, it is helpful to be bold, authentic, and just honest about how you feel.

Name Calling

This tactic can actually lead to grounds for divorce. Some people have a deal breaker about name calling, so be careful because it can end a marriage. It really hits below the belt, so to speak, and can cause some real damage in several areas of the marriage, including trust and intimacy.

Couples can make many different types of communication snafus or pitfalls. Remarrying is the time to seek to understand them and create your own unique process to resolve them. We will explore some great options in our next chapter.

Exercise:

1) Notice the pitfalls you tend to fall into. Cite some examples:

____
____
____
____
____
____

2) Notice what you hear from your partner that triggers upset feelings for you.

____
____
____
____
____
____

Share your feelings with one another, not in an accusatory way, but just as something you notice. "Noticing" is a great way to express yourself when you want to point something out to your partner. Be conscious of your tone. Keep it neutral. You will get more understanding and information that way.

Read on for the solutions to communication pitfalls in our next chapter so you both can create a process that works better for you.

Chapter 7

INGREDIENT 5—TALKING POINTS: EXPERIENCING LOVING AND EFFECTIVE COMMUNICATION

*"I've learned that people will forget what you said,
people will forget what you did,
but people will never forget how you made them feel."*

— *Maya Angelou*

So after reading the previous chapter on communication pitfalls that cause conflict and upset, are you ready to learn some tools to communicate more effectively? Imagine if communication went so smoothly that your conflicts were minimized. What would your marriage be like? I know I couldn't wait to get better at communication when I married Rick. Rick and I have amazing communication because we use these tools, and I know you can have the same results. Learning these tools and taking the time to practice them, even if it all initially sounds "fakey-fakey," will move you into a natural flow of graceful and effective ways of speaking, listening, and sharing so you will feel so much better about it all. It will feel more authentic as you practice.

As the quote above says, people will best remember how they feel around you so your words to one another will evoke an emotional reaction, and having a positive reaction will evoke positive and more loving feelings, which will make everything turn out much better for both of you. Learning these specific tools can help you to use words to communicate in a way that evokes more understanding, compassion, and ultimately, a stronger bond.

So, let's look at tools that can help with the following issues:

1. The Blame Game
2. Always & Never
3. Right & Wrong
4. Listening

And lead us to our ultimate goal: Practicing the Lost Art of Positive Communication.

Blame Game Tools

- **Use your "I" and "Me" Statements.**

What are those? Instead of saying to your partner "You made me feel so angry," try this:

"I felt angry when you said ________. It felt bad to me when you didn't_____________."

Why does that make a difference? It makes a difference because the *ownership* (which we will speak more about) of the anger is on the person who is sharing it. Using "I" statements and "me" statements takes the energy off of blaming your partner and allows you to own the fact that you feel or think the way you do.

Projecting how you feel or believe onto your partner as if he or she is (or even could possibly be) causing you to feel or think as you do is just not based in accuracy. Using "I" and "Me" statements creates communication that is being personally owned, so the other partner is less likely to feel attacked and blamed. There can be a request attached to it if you are asking your partner to alter, shift, or change something; we will get into how to make a request later in this chapter.

Always & Never Tools

Remember that *always* and *never* are not usually accurate words, so they can trigger a massive conflict. As I mentioned in the last chapter, people love to use these words to make their point, but it only adds to the mess.

Take the *always* and *never* out, and if you want to quantify, be accurate. Use words such as:

- Occasionally
- Sometimes
- A few times
- On occasion
- Here and there
- Frequently
- On several occasions
- Many times
- Now and again
- Most of the time

This way, while you may still be coming from a place of feeling upset, at least you are more accurate about your statement with less drama attached to it. This tool will make it easier to resolve the situation because this form of communication offers a way to quantify without being so extreme.

Example:

Beverly: Biff, I noticed that you forgot to get the car washed. I feel bad saying this, but I've noticed that on occasion, I will ask you to do something and it doesn't get done; what's going on with that?

Notice how Bev is using her "I" statements (points for you, Bev). She's also doing something else important that we will cover shortly.

Biff: I'm really sorry, Bev. I had intended to get the car washed, and I know I occasionally don't get those types of things done. When I have a long day at work,

> I just get tired and want to get home as quickly as possible, especially to spend time with you and the kids. I did have a longer meeting than expected today. Do you mind if I get it done tomorrow?
>
> (Way to go, Biff!)
>
> Beverly: It's fine, Biff, really. I appreciate you acknowledging that you sometimes don't get things done, and sure, get the car washed tomorrow. I know what an exhausting job you have, and I love that you want to get home to me.

See, isn't that better? Being more truthful about quantifying the time softened up the conversation.

Right & Wrong Tools

Instead of "right and wrong," I encourage you to consider two words:

- **Accurate and Inaccurate**

Why do I encourage you to use those words? Because they are based on being *factual* and they don't have the connotation of superiority, demand, or being bad and wrong. No one wants to be "inaccurate" either, but there is less of a sense of "bad" associated with it. It is a more neutral term.

Let's look at this conversation. Wilma and Fred (yes, I loved *The Flintstones*, too) are driving in the car to a wedding.

Here, Wilma could tell Fred, "You're going the wrong way," but look at how the conversation flows because she chooses different words.

> Wilma: Fred, I don't think this is the way to the wedding.
>
> Fred: Yes, honey, it is. Don't worry; I'm sure it's accurate.
>
> Wilma: Based on the Google Maps on my iPhone, this looks inaccurate to me.
>
> Fred: It doesn't look accurate? Okay, let's pull over and take a look and make sure we are going the best way.
>
> (Okay, well, right and wrong may be able to be used in that scenario, but let's look at this one.)
>
> Fred: Wilma, you told me that Biff and Beverly were coming over Saturday night for dinner. (Cool, these couples know each other!) I had it written down in my calendar, but Biff just told me it's next Saturday night. Which is one is accurate?
>
> Wilma: No, Fred, this Saturday night is not accurate; our dinner with them is next Saturday night.
>
> Fred: Well, then we are double-booked. I have us going to Bob and Sue McKellan's party that night.
>
> Wilma: Oh, Fred, honey, that's sadly not accurate ei-

ther. *This* Saturday night is the McKellans' party.
Fred: I could swear I had this written down accurately. Are you sure? I feel like I'm getting old here.

Wilma: Aww, Fred, you are just fine. We can go over the calendars together from now on so we make sure we both have accurate information.

See, here Fred might feel a little off, but Wilma was not making him wrong. There was no right or wrong war going on. There are moments when it is tempting to use the terms *right* and *wrong*, but if the intention is to feel superior or make your partner wrong, it's best to refrain and use *accurate* or *inaccurate* instead so that the conversation will not erupt into conflict.

Listening Tools

- **Reflecting Back**:

Reflecting back is simply allowing your partner to be fully heard after he or she speaks. It is getting as close to repeating back what you heard the other person say as close to verbatim as possible. Repeating back the essence of what you heard can work as well.

Example:

Barney: You know, Betty, my feelings were hurt last night when you were spending extra time with the kids and got too tired to spend any time with me.

Betty: So what I hear you saying, Barney, is that your feelings got hurt when I was too tired to spend some quality time with you. Is that accurate?

Barney: Yes, that is accurate.

In the first part of this process, there is no responding with an explanation, a defense, or an excuse yet, even though I know you're dying to! This first part is called *perception checking*. It is simply deep listening and reflecting back in your response what was said. We want to make sure we hear things accurately, which is why we need to ask, "Is that accurate?" By reflecting back, we can make sure we understand the facts vs. our interpretation of them. Being heard is critical to resolving any conflict and to communicating effectively. In general, a conversation or a request about something mundane like, "Honey, can you get the newspaper?" doesn't necessarily require the need to reflect back, but periodically, it is a good idea to reflect back when your partner is trying to share something that seems more important, especially when he or she is feeling triggered about something and wants to sort it out with you.

Often, the interpretation isn't as bad as you thought it was, and it diffuses the conflict right there in that moment. However, at times, it is what we thought we heard that brings forward our own trigger. When we feel triggered, we can fall back on using our I/Me statements that we covered earlier to express how we are feeling or how we respond to what was said. Remember, I/Me statements allow us to take ownership of our thoughts, feelings, and behaviors instead of making it about the other person.

More I/Me Statements:

- I hear you.
- I hear that that is how you saw things.
- I get it, or I got it.
- I feel like you are saying ___________.
- Here is how I interpreted what was happening.
- This is how it was occurring for me.
- This is what I thought was happening.
- I didn't realize that is how you felt.
- I feel that you ___________.
- I hear how that was for you.
- I hear how that must have sounded for you.
- I felt triggered when _________.
- What is coming forward for me is ______________.
- This is how it landed for me.
- It would help me out if you would ____________. (Making a request using an I/Me statement)

- I'm not clear about that. Would you repeat that, please?
- Perhaps I'm not sharing this well. I'll try again. (Assume that you did not deliver the message adequately, so try again rather than assuming your partner is an idiot who cannot understand.)

Here is a different version of the Blame Game conversation from our previous chapter using I/Me statements:

> Marge: "Hey, Steve, this is tough for me to share, but I felt really sad when I didn't get flowers on Valentine's Day.
>
> Steve: I thought a diamond necklace would make you smile. I went to several stores to find the most beautiful one for my beautiful wife. I'm so sorry that I didn't ask you what you would like; I really hear that you are saying you would have loved flowers in addition to the diamonds and that you are sad about that. Is that accurate? I really had good intentions, and I thought you'd like the diamond necklace better.
>
> Marge: Yes, it is accurate, and don't get me wrong; that necklace was so stunning and I do love it. I hear how much thought you put into it. Thank you, honey; I really love and appreciate it. For some reason, not getting flowers had me feeling sad as well. I am trying to look at what it brought forward for me to bring up such sadness. Again, I do appreciate your thoughtfulness, and I may have overreacted about not getting the flowers.

Steve: I'm sorry you feel sad about not getting the flowers. I really hear that and appreciate that you are searching for what that is really about for you. I thought about it and considered it, but I know how much you like diamonds, so I felt that the diamond necklace would really express my love for you and put a big smile on your face.

Marge: Yes, Steve, that was very thoughtful. I really appreciate you remembering that I love my diamonds! Again, I hear how much you were thinking of me and that is so sweet. I also hear that you did think of flowers as well, and while I felt sad that I didn't get them, I appreciate that you thought of them. Always know I love flowers with anything you get me. You can count on a big smile on my face with that.

Steve: What I hear you saying, Marge, is that no matter what else I want to get you, flowers are also something you love. Is that accurate?

Marge: Absolutely. Thank you for hearing me.

In this exchange, Marge was simply sharing her feelings rather than blaming Steve, and Steve responded very consciously as well. Marge was then able to appreciate what Steve had done for her, and Steve was not feeling blamed or attacked; he was simply explaining how much he thought about it, and he didn't feel the need to be on the defensive; he didn't react like he had been blamed or attacked, so the conversation went smoothly. Steve now has a deeper understanding of what Marge likes to receive, and he wasn't made wrong for not getting the flowers. He actually received appreciation from Marge.

Expressing Compassion, Empathy, and Validation

The tool of Reflecting Back can also have some add-ons that allow someone not only to be heard, but to be validated with a sense of compassion as well.

Expressing empathy can be expressed by saying, "I'm hearing that you are sad. I am so sorry you feel that way." Validation can happen by adding, "I can see how that would bring up sadness, knowing how much flowers mean to you." This type of response can allow such a conversation to be even more peaceful, loving, and bond-creating. Take the conversation to a deeper sense of understanding and compassion and you will notice better bonding through communication.

The Lost Art of Positive Communication

Man, are we a culture focused on what is wrong, or what? We are inundated with negativity—bad news on TV, the Internet, the radio, commercials, and even in our own minds. My professors from grad school, Drs. Ron and Mary Hulnick, taught me that we have the power to imagine our own future. Since we have that power, we might as well "win" in our own future fantasy.

Our minds tend to be on the hunt for what's not working in life and in marriage, especially if there is a painful history.

They have a hard time imagining a bright and beautiful future, so we have to work at that. I have been told by clients several times that they are waiting for "the other shoe to drop" when things are good.

My response? "What if the other shoe is a Manolo?" If you don't know this ladies shoe, look it up. My point is that the other shoe can be amazing, and we don't have to wait for the bad to happen.

So while our minds are busy searching for the negative, they are also busy looking for negative words to use instead of ways they can acknowledge, appreciate, express love, compliment, and really praise (or prize) our partners.

When I mentioned earlier that there are moments to use the word "you" to start the sentence, this is it!

- You look mahvelous!
- I so appreciate you!
- You are the love of my life!
- You look beautiful!
- You look so handsome in that suit.
- I just love you for you!
- You are the person I always dreamed about and wished for.
- I am so grateful for you.

- Thank you!
- You are so awesome!

Beautiful words of acknowledgment, appreciation, love, and praise never get old! Both my husband and I love words, so the amount of beautiful cards, emails, texts, and Post-it notes we have exchanged over the years have not only brought our relationship closer, but they could literally mural a huge wall! It makes such an impact when you remember to say something positive daily to your partner. If you are angry and can't come up with anything that day, at least tell your partner you are grateful that he or she is still breathing. Hopefully, you will have more than that to share.

So these last two chapters have been just samples of how to improve your communication. There are a lot more methods and examples I could share. In my private coaching practice and in virtual classes, online programs, and speeches I offer, I teach these communication skills because they are a critical part of remarrying right and creating everlasting love with your true soul mate.

Learn them, practice them, and apply them to your marriage. Also, read the next two chapters to absorb fully and apply even more skills that will help. Then take time to notice and enjoy how much more harmony and love you are experiencing together.

Exercise:

My default communication tendencies (be honest, now):

What I am committed to changing, practicing, and applying:

Chapter 8

INGREDIENT 6—OWNING YOUR ONCE UPON A TIME

"What a liberation it is to realize that the ' voice in my head' is not who I am. Who am I then? The one who sees that."

— Eckhart Tolle

I so love a good story; don't you? Can you think of some of your favorite movies, TV shows, and books? Are you a fan of thrillers, romance, horror, drama, comedy? Personally, I am into the young adult genre, despite my age, along with some good PG supernatural stories and the superhero ones as well. Then we have the rom-coms—the Hallmark channel romances where the couple finally gets together during the last thirty seconds of the movie. Do we really have to wait that long? We know how Hallmark movies are going to end.

Now think of your own life story. Yeah, the mood just changed there, didn't it? We all have our life stories, but the stories I'm referring to in this chapter are the stories, programs, and limiting beliefs we all carry that are guaranteed to pop up in our marriage. Here are some of the stories I'm referring to:

- I'm not good enough.
- I'm not important enough.
- I just can't win.
- Nothing ever goes right for me.
- I never get what I want.
- I'll never really be happy.
- I'm not loveable.
- I'm a loser.
- No one really loves me.
- I can't do that.
- I'll never get this right.
- I'll never be successful.
- My life sucks.
- I'm not attractive enough.

- I'm not smart enough.
- My spouse made me angry, upset, feel bad, look bad, feel dumb, etc.
- I can't because __________________. (Some outside force)
- I'm upset because __________________. (Some outside force)
- My spouse might leave me.
- Being alone is the worst thing ever.
- Our marriage will never make it.
- I'm not pretty enough.
- I'm not important enough.
- My dog ate my homework. (Okay, that's from my years of teaching high school.)

Shall I continue? I could go on and on for pages and pages. Imagine when we are young children, around four to six years old, that are minds are like little computers being programmed with software that we will install and have for years and years until we delete it.

Imagine you are four years old and playing a game with your mom when the phone rings. She gets up to answer the phone in the other room and doesn't come back for a while. In that moment, it is easy to start imagining negative reasons why she doesn't come back, and those ideas can carry over into your adult life. Here's how it would work:

- **The Fact:** The phone rang and Mom went to answer it.
- **The Interpretation (What I made it mean):** She doesn't want to play with me.
- **The Deeper Story:** She abandoned me.
- **The Hook:** Now I feel people will leave me.
- **The Experiences:** So many people have come in and then walked out of my life.
- **The Feelings:** I feel sad, angry, scared.
- **The Negative Future Story:** People will leave me.
- **The Relationship Experience:** People dump me.
- **The First Marriage Experience:** My spouse passed away and left me, or my spouse divorced me, or my spouse betrayed me so I had to get a divorce.
- **My Current (or Soon-to-Be) Marriage Belief/Fear:** My spouse might leave me.

My Behavior as a Result of This Belief: I must do everything to protect myself and act as if my spouse will leave. I need to communicate from that assumption, take it out on my spouse, and project onto my spouse from the wounds of my past.

Another term for this behavior is a "competing or dueling intention." The intention of being happily married again is competing with the negative stories, which causes internal conflict.

This example reflects the power of the stories we tell ourselves. They are guaranteed to come forward in a marriage, especially a second or third marriage, because the stories were triggered in the previous marriage, whether through projections, thoughts, behavior, or words. Often, people are not always aware of the stories on a conscious level so they act on them without understanding where the words, thoughts, beliefs, feelings, and behaviors are coming from. The first step to understanding them and how they are affecting the marriage is to bring them up to conscious awareness. There are several ways to do this. First, you can create a list of what you do know about your own stories. You can start here:

My main default stories:

____

____

____

____

____

Triggering events in my life and what I made them mean:

____

____

____

____

____

Negative experiences in my life that have me puzzled:

____
____
____
____
____
____

Projections I have made on my partner because he/she said or did something that triggered a story:

____
____
____
____
____
____
____

Insights into stories that may have previously been hidden:

____
____
____
____
____
____
____

These are some powerful inquiries. Sit with them for a while and see what comes up. Once we look at known stories based on events in our lives and our behaviors, beliefs, and thoughts, we can then look at tools to help clear them.

Clearing Tools

What are clearing tools? They are techniques that not only help you clear old stories, programming, and beliefs, but also bring hidden ones up to the surface. Imagine for a moment that the stories of your life are stuffed in a tissue box. Some that are close to or at the surface you may be aware of, but then there are many tissues stuck at the bottom that you may not know are there, even though they may have been there for decades.

Clearing techniques help you notice which "tissue" is popping up at the surface, so you can gently grab it and release it. After a while, you will feel lighter and notice the change in your mental space. Your behaviors and thoughts may shift, and the way you project onto your partner may also change. Then life in your household may be more harmonious, more fun, and more loving.

But then what happens? The next tissue or tissues stuck together pop up. Then we may feel the story again or the negative feelings. What do we do? We use one of these techniques to whisk it away again. The lightness returns, and you may see your external reality shift even more. You may see your marriage feeling more bonded, close, and intimate than it was before. Your partner may even behave differently (in a good way) with you because he or she feels the change in your energy. If you are both using the clearing techniques, the marriage gets even better. You both may go through periods of time feeling what tissues are popping up, but once cleared, the lightness of life and love gets even better.

So let's look at two clearing techniques in detail:

1. The Sedona Method
2. EFT (Emotional Freedom Technique)

The Sedona Method®

The Sedona Method is a simple, yet powerful technique to assist you in letting go of or releasing unwanted thoughts, feelings, stories, and reactions to negative memories. Memories will stay, but using the Sedona Method will allow you to experience less of a negative reaction to them. Explaining how the Sedona Method works is like trying to explain how it feels finally to get to drive a car or ride a bicycle. It has to be experienced.

Here, from the Sedona Training Associates website with Hale Dwoskin (sedona.com), is a bit of an explanation to explain the unexplainable:

> The Sedona Method is a unique, simple, powerful, easy-to-learn and duplicate technique that shows you how to uncover your natural ability to let go of any painful or unwanted feeling in the moment. The Sedona Method consists of a series of questions you ask yourself that lead your awareness to what you are feeling in the moment and gently guide you into the experience of letting go.

What makes the Sedona Method a powerful tool (that really works!) is that it is a process you can use anytime, anyplace, to improve any area of your life. Plus, no one will know you are doing it!

> Best of all, the Sedona Method helps you to focus on achieving your goals. It allows you to clear the past or, in terms of goal-setting, to clear negative anticipatory thoughts and images we create about the future. By focusing on your future and setting and achieving your goals for the future, you can dramatically shift your mindset from the past. Plus, achieving the future you want will help you to heal your past. The benefits you experience will include:
>
> - Dramatic shifts in self-esteem and self-confidence that will improve your career, ignite passionate romances, create wealth, launch businesses, and much more.
> - Deep feelings of inner peace that bring more joy and happiness to everyday life.
> - Freedom from long-standing emotional challenges such as fear and anxiety, anger management, depression, and emotional traumas.
> - Courage to take massive action toward being, doing, and having the most exciting things life has to offer.
> - Putting an end, once and for all, to the struggle to quit smoking, drinking, overeating, or engaging in other impulsive, addictive, and self-defeating behaviors.

This is just the tip of the iceberg. I personally use the Sedona Method in my life, and I use it professionally with my coaching clients. I have been trained to coach this method, and I feel it is one of the best techniques out there because it works with any area of life, and it works really well with relationships.

I highly recommend exploring this technique together with your partner. What I like about it is the statement that it can be used anytime and anyplace. Why? Because it is a very internal process, so no one knows you are doing it. It can be effective in one session, but most of us have layers of stories, so I recommend learning this technique and using it as you need to or as a practice.

Check out www.sedona.com to see whether it resonates. Again, I use this method with clients during sessions and encourage them to use it between sessions. For a husband and wife, it can be used together to work through and release stories that contribute to a conflict, or it can be used to help achieve a goal.

When my husband and I used the Sedona Method to manifest our current home, we ended up with our dream—buying a slab of land where our home would be built. We got to watch the process and to choose the paint color, flooring, carpeting, countertops, etc. It was a dream come true to go through that process, pick out new furniture, and create our backyard from scratch. We credit using the Sedona method for opening us up to allowing this to happen because we both wanted a house that was built from the ground up. We got the square footage we wanted and a layout that we love, and we are grateful every day that the Sedona Method helped us clear whatever stories we had inside that otherwise would have prevented us from getting a home like this.

I have seen clients use this method to create harmony at home, achieve their individual goals and dreams, and also manifest their dreams together. It's very powerful to use it to let layers of negative thoughts and feelings go forever and be at peace.

It is so easy to do that you won't really get how something so simple can be so powerful, but it is!

EFT (Emotional Freedom Technique) or Tapping

EFT is more of a "doing" process, so movement is involved. It is an external process that involves using your fingers to tap on specific meridian points on the body in a specific sequence, while speaking your concerns, issues, stories, goals, and dreams for the future out loud. For example, your issues might be dealing with grief, jealousy, anxiety, pain, or fear after a traumatic event like a car accident, or retelling yourself the story of a bad incident you experienced. You can use specific sequences of tapping on the specific meridian points while you share your emotions or traumatic event, or even your goal, and it will help wash away the pain and release the suffering. It is another great tool for relationships; individual pursuits; releasing old issues, patterns, and beliefs; clearing old wounds; physical pain relief; and so much more. I am also trained to facilitate it.

For more information about EFT or Tapping, its history, process, sequences, and benefits, check out www.thetappingsolution.com. It is my personal favorite website when it comes to tapping. You can also go to You Tube and type in "EFT" and a topic you wish to work with (for example "EFT and jealousy") and find a lot of great short videos. My favorite EFT experts are Nick and Jessica Ortner. They have several videos at YouTube that take you through the process and show you where and how to tap while speaking your challenge or goal. You will find that tapping and the Sedona Method leave you feeling lighter about your challenge and closer to obtaining your goals. Things can shift quickly, or they may take a while, so be patient with these techniques and be diligent as the more you release or tap, the lighter you feel and the closer you are to obtaining your goals.

I offer both the Sedona Method and EFT so I can give interested clients an experience of both so they can see which resonates for them. Some clients try one and take to it immediately, so they don't feel the need for the other. In my personal life, I use both, depending on where I am and what I am in the mood for. I have used these techniques for business, health, relationships, goals, and family moments (Can we all relate?), and I love both techniques. One thing I like about having multiple options is that when I am in public, I will do the Sedona Method. In private, I can choose either.

Again, my clients tend to gravitate to one or the other, and some like both. In a marriage, both partners can use either and can even facilitate each other through the process. This not only helps with clearing issues, old stories, goals, etc., but also with connection and intimacy when a couple works through these techniques together.

Of course, couples can use other techniques as well. These just happen to be my favorites and the most effective ones I have used.

Imagine creating more tranquility, intimacy, love, support, and peace between the two of you and individually inside of you than you have ever imagined! Imagine letting go of the story of your previous marriage and anything you are still lugging around inside about it! Wow! Freedom!

Chapter 9

INGREDIENT 7—PLAYING NICE

"Many marriages would be better if the husband and wife clearly understood that they are on the same side."

— Zig Ziglar

Growing up, did anyone ever teach you how to resolve conflict with other people? Yeah, me neither. My first marriage was filled with a ton of conflict, arguments, the desire for the other person to change (drastically, at least on my end), and constant frustration with each other. I had an enormous amount of internal conflict—feelings of betrayal, hurt, anger, and pain—because the marriage was just not working. We didn't resolve disagreements well because we didn't have the language or skills to do so. During that marriage, I was fortunate enough to take a certification course in conflict resolution. In fact, I took several courses, intending to bring it to my students while I was a teacher since it was the latest trend in schools at that time. So, in the last chapter we talked about taking personal ownership, and this topic leads us into how to resolve conflict and why taking ownership is important.

It did occur to me to apply conflict resolution to my marriage to see how it could work given the issues we had. Sadly, I felt I had an unwilling partner at the time so it would be no use. I didn't feel the marriage would improve without him having a desire to do his part, so I knew at that point that I would ultimately end up divorced. There were just too many deal breakers that happened, yet it took me a while following the first one to decide to divorce him.

Today, I have become a woman who wouldn't have married a man like him in the first place. I don't say that because he is a bad person; I just mean today I would have seen the blazing red flags at the beginning of our dating process. I would have honored the higher standards I now have for a relationship and would have ended the relationship within the first month.

Most couples come to me believing their real conflict is what they are presenting on a surface level. For example, one couple I worked with several times needed help because they'd just had a new baby. The wife (I'll call her Rochelle) was able to stay home and care for her child, but it was a busier and more challenging experience than she had imagined. She loved her baby, but she was exhausted. Her husband (I'll call him Paul) worked all day outside of the home and came home to find dishes not done and a few other things in the house in disarray. He would get very triggered by this and couldn't understand why things in the house weren't done. They were both in their second marriage, but it was their first time being parents. Like many people, they didn't know what to expect as new parents, but Paul thought since Rochelle was home all day, she could easily do the household chores. On the weekends, Paul took over the morning duties with their baby and Rochelle got to sleep in. On occasion, however, when they would attend an event or go out with friends on the weekends, Rochelle would have to wake up Paul to make sure he was ready on time. After this happened a few times, Rochelle came to resent the fact that Paul couldn't get himself ready on time. After all, a lot of preparation was needed to bring their baby with them, and Paul had committed to being in charge of that on the weekends, but he wasn't being consistent.

When I spoke with Paul and Rochelle, I immediately knew the conflict wasn't really about the dishes or about Paul not being ready on time. It was about what was beneath the surface issues.

Conflicts rarely are about what is presented on the surface. Surface issues can bring up some frustration, but the real issues lie much deeper.

I tell the couples I work with that it isn't really about the dishes. It's about what we make the surface issue mean. How we respond or relate to the issue is the *real* issue.

So, what are some underlying issues that the conflict or triggers are really about?

Generally, the reason we have conflict is because we are lugging around those stories I mentioned in the previous chapter. What happens is quite common. Our partner says or does something, mostly unintentionally, and it just so happens that we have a trigger that comes up. For example, when Paul gets home and sees that the dishes are not done, he feels he is not being cared for. This feeling can be traced back to his early upbringing. Every time he didn't feel cared for, it was like being programmed with that "software" over and over again. It happened to the degree that it activated a trigger inside of him that could have been brought forward by several things. For Rochelle, when Paul wasn't ready, she felt unimportant.

Then, of course, there is an emotional reaction to the thought, belief, or story that gets triggered. This emotional reaction is what ignites the conflict.

So let's summarize the process:

- An event happens
- Someone's story gets triggered (It's like stepping on someone's hidden landmine.)
- Reactive emotions come forward and get expressed—whether expressed outwardly, or by someone shutting down inwardly
- Conflict begins because both parties are now in "upset" mode

When this kind of situation occurs, check inside to see whether the conflict is really about the event that happened or the reaction and response to that event. Dishes could be left in the sink without either partner having any negative response. Both could just say, "They will be done in the morning" and the evening goes on. For others, the dishes trigger something deeper, and when the emotions get expressed or the shut down happens, it also triggers something in the other person, and both are now in the heat of conflict. The challenge is getting to the real issue about the conflict and working through that rather than arguing about the surface event. It is also important to understand the real stories that got triggered and work through them. Here is also where personal ownership comes in. We have to take ownership for the stories, feelings, emotions, and behaviors we have, even if we feel someone else triggered them. This is the most challenging part of conflict resolution because we are so tempted to blame the other person, even though the stories that get triggered have been living inside of us since we were young, long before we met any spouse.

So here is an overview of a process that can help you resolve conflict. The key to resolving conflict is to maintain a level of awareness in the midst of being in a highly emotional reaction space.

- Identify the event—state the facts: What actually happened?
- Identify the story about it: What did you make it mean?
- Identify the emotions triggered by the story: How did it make you feel?

- Identify past experiences with similar events: When was the first time you felt this way? What was the original triggering event?
- Identify what you can take ownership about.
- Identify what you'd like to see happen moving forward: What would be ideal for you?
- Identify any reasonable requests you have of your partner. Share them.
- Hear your partner's point of view, story, feelings, old triggers, gentle requests.
- Negotiate to find common ground.
- Create a plan moving forward.
- Release and clear any remaining negative emotions you still have.

This process can be very effective when working with a coach, of course, but with practice, it also can be done effectively at home. It takes patience, understanding, ownership, compassion, trust, a reminder that you love the other person, a willingness to seek resolution and common ground, and a willingness to recognize that the story and feelings triggered have been living inside of you. Your partner merely accidentally stepped on that "landmine."

Now it's time to try it out:

Exercise:

The Event (What happened):

My story about the event (What I made it mean):

How it made me feel:

When I remember feeling that way earlier in my life:

What the triggering event was back then:

____

____

____

____

____

____

What I can own about the experience:

____

____

____

____

____

____

What I would like to see happen:

____

____

____

____

____

____

Reasonable requests I would like to make of my partner:

____

____

____

____

____

____

My understanding of my partner's viewpoint, stories, feelings, old triggers, and requests:

Our negotiated plan moving forward:

What I need to release and clear inside myself:

Any resistance to our plan:

What we need to release or course correct moving forward:

____

____

____

____

____

____

The success of our plan:

____

____

____

____

____

____

This process takes patience, practice, and time. But it will also bring harmony back into your marriage. If you are about to remarry, bring in harmony as you enter this beautiful journey! Remember that conflict is really about one partner's story hitting the other partner's story. If conflict cannot be resolved, then the conflict is likely based on a deal breaker, and that is an unfortunate situation that likely won't have a great resolution. Conflict that can be resolved is based on a power struggle between core essential needs, but it won't destroy the marriage or prevent the marriage from happening.

What kind of conflict is it?

What are your options if it is based on a deal breaker? Likely, there are two outcomes: 1) stay in the marriage (or get married) and sacrifice your deal breaker, or 2) leave the marriage (or don't get married to this person). Unfortunately, those are the only options.

Try the exercise first and see what is possible.

Chapter 10

INGREDIENT 8—LETTING SHIT GO

"Feelings only lie. They tell you that you are going to get from letting go of them what you already have from holding onto them."

— Hale Dwoskin

I have this really challenging habit of being an over-packer whenever I travel. Like many women, I seem to need several options for clothing to wear because I want to have choices, and I seem to feel the need to bring things for the "just in case" moments. It's not like I'm going camping, though. I travel to civilized places where, if I forgot something, I could easily run to a store and buy it. Despite that fact, I also think, "What if my luggage doesn't make it?" So I pile things into my carry-on bags. In short, I don't travel light; I over-pack, over-think, and end up carrying way too much with me, and I do it based on the "what if" fear stories that come up.

Meanwhile, Rick throws a couple of shirts in his carry-on, along with his sundries, a brush and hair dryer, a couple of pairs of pants, shoes, socks, and undies, and calls it a day.

Anyone else have this experience? Are you an over-packer? Is this a gender thing? Taking ownership and resolving conflict are even more effective when you can become aware of the baggage you carry. You don't have to know every piece of it; you just need to know which items are affecting you now.

Well, in life, we all have over-packed our stories, our limiting beliefs, our patterns, etc., and we hold on to them with a death grip as if letting go will suddenly bring forward our demise.

So how can we just let that shit go and allow ourselves to go with the flow, creating a new story rather than fearing what might happen? Let's be honest; when we married before, bad things happened, so more fear got stored. We fear that "what ifs" can happen in this marriage as well, especially because of the last one.

Letting go of this fear isn't easy because the ego thinks that by holding on, we will protect ourselves, while by letting go, everything will fall apart and we won't get what we want.

In actuality (and you can check this out for yourself), it is the exact opposite.

As Hale Dwoskin, leader of the Sedona Training Associates, says, "You can't sit down and stand up at the same time." (Try it). Would we rather have what we want, or want what we don't have? Holding on is fear-based. We hold on to ideas, thoughts, beliefs, stories, and negative emotions out of fear.

To be in flow with the universe, and in harmony in our relationships, we need to let things go. That includes past relationship events, stories about them, family of origin events, our stories about them, the upper limit we tend to place on ourselves that limits how good things can be, and the idea that because something happened in the past, it will happen in our future. There are so many things to let go of, and one blessing about the Sedona Method as well as EFT is that we don't have to go into recall of every event and emotion in our lives in order to let go of it. (Thank God.)

Are you someone who thinks that what happened in your past marriage—whether you have been divorced, widowed, or even formerly engaged (and are marrying or are married to someone who has been married before)—is an indicator of what will happen in the future?

I have a client who has been formerly engaged but is still single. She wants to manifest marriage, and because she is in her late forties, she will likely meet and marry someone who has been married before. One challenge she has that so many others have is the assumption that what happened before will happen again. I've addressed this issue previously in this book, but I want to address it more deeply since it is a very common way of thinking. Since we don't always know what the future will bring, we tend to look at what happened before and decide it will happen again because we can't see what's ahead.

So letting go is really about letting go of "what was"—the stories you have had about how things used to be—and deciding that the future doesn't have to be that way.

If you used to be in a marriage with someone who lied and cheated, and perhaps, had a few previous relationships like that, it doesn't mean it will happen again. We tend to start creating the idea that we have a pattern. We may or may not, but even if we do, that doesn't mean the pattern is unbreakable. A pattern doesn't have to be your lot in life. Many people are just waiting for the past to happen again, and again, almost wanting, looking for, and expecting it to happen so they can unconsciously defend and prove their story to be accurate. In this fearful mindset, they aren't paying attention to what is *actually* happening.

Without question, changing the experience means changing the story, and changing the story involves letting the old shit go about what happened in the past so the future looks more like a blank canvas and you have all the paint you need to co-create it with your partner. Co-creating a future (from my viewpoint) is more about listening to deep inner wisdom than trying to come up with something just to have something.

What do I mean by that? I believe we co-create with our Higher Power, whether you call it God, Spirit, the Universe, Source, or something else. If you aren't a super-spiritual person, the universe is usually a fair way of looking at what is beyond our human experience. I believe it is a matter of connecting with that Higher Power, which is the higher version of ourselves, and listening deeply. Once we hear or get the nudge about something we want to see for our future, we can write it down and begin to take conscious, intuitive action toward it.

From my perspective, "listening" means that we just don't have complete control of it all when it comes to life or love. We have some say in the action steps we take and the way we imagine our future, but I believe some things are already meant for and waiting for us; however, in order for there to be room in our lives for them, first we need to let go of some things so we can embrace what's next.

Let me give you an example of this from my own life. I believe that even if I had not married my first husband and had married someone else, I would have gone through a similar experience with a man who lied and cheated. Why? Because I believe I had some unhealthy stories and beliefs about myself, my relationships, and my marriage. The way this came to my attention was to have an experience of betrayal. I would have loved just to get a memo that said, "Oh, by the way, please value yourself more, 'kay?" I mean, that would have been great and a hell of a lot easier, but would it have been as powerful or impactful? I honestly don't know. What was impactful and a huge catalyst for my growth was being in a marriage with a man who lied, cheated, and did things that lacked integrity and were breaches in the commitment he had made to me. As I mentioned before, it wasn't my first trip to that rodeo either, so it certainly got my attention.

Betrayal was a painful way to be notified that I needed to course correct and change my story about myself. I wouldn't wish that experience on anyone, but it provided me with such pain that many of my old stories and beliefs about myself that I was carrying came flying out of me. Rather than continue this pattern in relationship after relationship, I had to realize I was the common denominator in my past marriage and previous relationships.

My next step as I started to "unpack" and let some of that shit go was to enter a new relationship that told me things had improved, but my growth in this area wasn't quite finished. I knew there was more to do and more for me to learn, so I dove into more personal growth programs and explored more reading material so I could learn. I was quite determined to unpack and let go so I could have the marriage I wanted. And I did. Thank goodness! The best part of co-creating is that when we envision what we want, we make a request from the universe: "This or something better for the highest good of all concerned." I am now sure I got the something better with my second husband—no question about it.

Why do we add the "something better" phrase? Well, our human minds have a limited capacity to imagine what is possible, so we want our energy to open up and expand in order to receive the highest and best for us, so if we don't come up with the "something better" idea in our minds and hearts, then it will be revealed through the One Mind—through Source, God/Spirit—and hit us like a sledgehammer again.

So many people are incredibly fearful that their pasts will be their futures. Letting all of that shit go (or as much as possible) is the way to prevent that from happening.

Isn't it time to start unpacking that very heavy luggage set you have been carrying, filled with your negative stories, limiting beliefs, emotional reactions to what was (and more), and to keep that suitcase set empty so it can be filled with what you will focus on co-creating for your own future and for your future with your spouse?

Exercise:

Letting go and co-creating the future can be a really fun bonding exercise with your spouse. So ask yourself:

What are you holding on to that is currently disturbing your inner peace?

____
____
____
____
____
____

What are you holding on to that is currently disturbing this marriage or the one you are about to step into?

____
____
____
____
____
____

What items are in that heavy luggage set that you know you need to let go of?

____

____

____

____

____

____

Envisioning Your New Love Story

Once you have let go and unpacked that beat up ol' luggage set, you can sit with your partner and do this exercise, or if you are divorced and single, but looking to manifest marriage, you can do this following powerful exercise on your own.

I suggest it be done together as a couple and then individually for yourself.

Start by writing a list in present tense starting with "I am" or "We are" and then adding what you want to create. Feel free to add words of inspiration such as:

- We are thoroughly enjoying our annual visits to Tuscany.
- We are feeling so blessed to have a marriage that is all we had dreamed of and more.
- We are enjoying living in our new home that is so filled with love.

Again, write the list for yourselves as a couple and write your list as an individual as well.

Then tell a new story about your future on a different piece of paper or create a vision board if you are visual. I recommend doing a vision board with corkboard, magazine cutouts, and thumb tacks. Why? It's just easier to make changes, and changes will occur as you move forward.

You can work on the letting go part using the techniques I described in a previous chapter, or you can create the new story first, but be aware that old energy will come up. Why does the old energy come up? First of all, it is ready to be released. Secondly, it increases the awareness of what has been sitting in that heavy luggage set and why it has been so over-packed.

Do all of the exercises above and give this a try. It is extremely effective and powerful.

What do you have to lose except crappy stories in a crappy luggage set?

Don't worry about the timing of things. It is common for people to wonder when things will happen, but let go of that desire for now as well. Make sure what you write is at least 50 percent believable.

Following the creation of your new story, be careful not to jump in and try to "make it all happen." Take action steps on your new story as ideas for action flow to you. They will come in as an idea, a nudge on what you can do, or they may even feel like a sledgehammer banging on your head if you didn't catch the gentle nudge.

And the most important thing to do is to listen. Listen deeply, not from your mind, but from what is beyond the mind and from your heart.

Listening is important because what you hear will be part of your next steps following the creation of your new story, and it is important to listen and feel your own sense of alignment with this new story and with the action steps that present themselves. As you gain clarity about the new story you want, remember to make course corrections as needed. Sometimes when we write a new story, we think something we have included is a brilliant idea at the time, but later, we look back at it and ask ourselves, "What the hell was I thinking?" If it no longer resonates, feel free to remove it. New story items can be changed. Don't be afraid to change something that doesn't feel right to you or that changes as time goes by.

So let's summarize this unpacking process so you have room for the new journey that awaits you:

1) Notice what you have been carrying around in that heavy luggage set.

2) Notice how it is affecting your marriage.

3) Notice (as best you can) what your partner is carrying and even have a discussion about it.

4) Work on researching and using the letting go techniques. Again, you can find free information on YouTube, and if you want to purchase anyone's products or attend any live event, go for it.

5) Write down in present tense the list of things you would like to see in your marriage and in your life in general.

6) Take that list and create a new story for your marriage and for your life. This can be a narrative or a vision board.

7) Look at potential action steps and determine whether they are coming to you from a deep, more intuitive level. If so, take one or more of the steps. If not, sit back and reevaluate.

8) Notice what happens. Hopefully, you can reduce or even throw out the heavy luggage set and look forward to a new future with your spouse or soon-to-be spouse and for your life.

9) Trust the timing. You have little control over it, so just go with the flow.

Chapter 11

INGREDIENT 9—BASKING IN THE HEAT OF THE NIGHT

"Real connection and intimacy is like a meal, not a sugar fix."

— Kristin Armstrong

Is intimacy going really well for you right now? Remarriage is an interesting space in regards to intimacy. Clearly, both partners have had all levels of intimacy prior to meeting each other, so there is a tendency for intimacy issues to come forward. In the last chapter, we talked about letting go of old patterns and rewriting your new story. In this chapter, we will explore how a new story may also need to be created in the area of intimacy.

As a coach, I find that intimacy is not an easy area to work with, not because I am uncomfortable with it, but because many couples have a challenging time sharing what is happening for them in this area. If all is well, that is great. If there is confusion, difficulty communicating about intimacy, disinterest, lack of connection, lack of emotional intimacy, or many other possible issues, it can be difficult, but regardless, there are solutions. In this chapter, we will look at those solutions and explore the concept of "wholistic intimacy," which allows for intimacy in multiple ways. Wholistic intimacy provides an overall fulfilling flow of intimacy in the marriage.

Most couples in their second and third marriages are in their midlife years. As a coach, the first step I take when intimacy is a challenge for a couple is to request that both partners get a medical check-up of their endocrine systems. Why? Well, it is common in our midlife years for hormones to change. Women may experience peri-menopause—menopause issues with hormones going haywire, that if not supplemented or supported, can cause a loss in sex drive and a lot of irritability, which may lead to conflict in the relationship. I recommend that men get their testosterone checked and that both partners get all hormones, thyroid, etc. checked because issues with them could explain why physical and emotional intimacy may not be going so well. Men can go through something called "andropause," which is a decline in testosterone, which will also contribute to a lack of sex drive.

Here are some other reasons physical and emotional intimacy may be compromised:

- Lack of emotional connection (sharing, connecting, expressing feelings)
- Lack of verbal sharing or conversation (Intellectual sharing and conversation about daily events create connection.)
- Lack of sexual foreplay ("Wham, bam, thank you, ma'am" isn't always appealing.)
- Lack of sex (Lack of any sex will divide a couple, and it is worse when there is a lack of communication about it.)
- Lack of chemistry (If chemistry isn't present, attraction isn't very present either.)
- Lack of romantic gestures (If people feel neglected, they won't feel the desire to be intimate.)
- Different sexual and emotional preferences (These require conversation and negotiation.)
- Sexual technique issues (Discuss and keep trying!)
- Feeling unheard (This feeling lowers levels of trust as well as connection.)
- Sexual frequency differences (These must be discussed and negotiated.)
- Lack of quality time together (Make the time!)
- Lack of expressing vulnerability (Keeping a wall up doesn't help intimacy.)

- Lack of verbal expressions of love (Most people like hearing positive things about themselves and words of love and affirmation.)
- Lack of verbal expressions of appreciation (Everyone wants to be acknowledged and appreciated.)
- Lack of household contribution: no sense of a team feeling (Feeling alone and that your partner isn't participating will reduce trust and foster resentment.)
- Opposite work schedules (Do your best to make any changes necessary or they will prevent time for intimacy.)
- Fear of rejection (This fear is very internal, but when not discussed, it can feel paralyzing.)
- Body image issues (This can be an internal issue, but it needs to be shared. Most people with these issues will be pleasantly surprised by how much their partner is attracted to them.)
- Medical issues (outside of what is mentioned above)
- Work hours (Too many work hours prevents quality time.)
- Kids (They require a lot of commitment; change the dynamic of the relationship and require some creative planning for intimacy.)
- Lack of physical touch
- Lack of creativity
- Lack of spontaneity

- Lack of planning
- Feeling unimportant or invisible
- Unresolved conflict
- Lack of compassion and tenderness
- Unresolved anger and frustration
- Misplaced priorities
- Self-centeredness
- Stories, limiting beliefs, and programs
- Poor general communication
- Lack of initiation
- Lack of interest
- Feelings of grief and loss (During times of grief, intimacy is not on the priority list, but it will come back.)
- Feelings of failure in life (Such feelings make connecting more challenging because self-esteem is low.)
- Infidelity (This is a major one, a deal breaker for many, which may end everything.)
- Lack of trust, integrity, and honesty (Lying and not keeping one's word will break down trust, which will kill intimacy.)
- Financial problems and struggle (These may ruin the entire relationship.)

- Avoidance and resistance of communication and connection
- Stress and exhaustion (These happen a lot to parents of younger kids.)
- Demand and obligation about being intimate (No one wants to feel coerced or controlled.)
- Lack of understanding (When people feel misunderstood, it is harder to connect.)
- Unhealed issues from the previous marriage
- Fears that you won't measure up sexually to the previous spouse.

Other, even more serious issues that will prevent emotional and physical intimacy include substance abuse; prior sexual abuse that has not been dealt with; other unhealed trauma; physical, emotional, or verbal abuse (from the past or in the marriage); and mental health disorders (in which case, therapy, psychiatry, and further medical intervention may be required to deal with them so the marriage can be brought back to an intimate and connected space.)

The most important first step is to talk about these issues. Talk about what isn't feeling right, what each person would like to see happen, and any issues from the past that may be interfering with intimacy in the present. It is also important to talk about any fears about intimacy from the previous marriage so they can remain in the past. Insecurities often get triggered, especially if the former spouse is in the picture due to co-parenting.

Wholistic Intimacy

Generally, when you think of intimacy, don't you think of sex? Most people do, but the concept of intimacy is much more than that. I call it "wholistic intimacy" to include:

- Physical Intimacy
- Emotional Intimacy
- Intellectual Intimacy
- Spiritual Intimacy

In the remainder of this chapter, I will explain each of these intimacies, how they can look in marriage, what happens if something is off, and how a couple can keep intimacy present in their marriage.

If you've been divorced, you know that something went awry in the area of intimacy on one or more of these levels in your previous marriage. It may not have been the deciding factor of the divorce, but there is generally a disconnection in the intimacy area in a marriage that ends in divorce.

For remarriage, a couple clearly wants their level of intimacy to be even better than their last marriage or relationship. In fact, many couples think that it's the new person who is creating a more exciting level of physical intimacy. While some of that may be accurate, it takes more than the excitement of a new person to sustain a lifelong connection.

Physical Intimacy

I don't think it's any mystery when I say that physical intimacy needs to be mutual, and even after the integration phase of the relationship, it needs to be maintained in a way that works for both partners. There is often a point in time when the physical intimacy fades a bit and certainly a time when the couple is much older when other priorities become more important. Physical intimacy, however, isn't just about sex. It is about touch, hand-holding, kissing, and just connecting in a physical way. Every couple is different, so physical intimacy gets to be created. This is a sensitive area, mostly due to the cultural pressures we have and the media onslaught of sex in magazines, movies, TV, etc. While most people enjoy a sexual connection in their marriage, how, when, and where often gets to be determined by the couple. Many sex experts make their recommendations, but it is truly up to the couple how they want their physical intimacy to be. If it is mutual and harmless, all is well. If it isn't, then there will be conflict around it. It is important to be able to discuss it inside of the partnership. Don't compare this marriage to your last one or your spouse to your previous one in the area of intimacy. Create intimacy together. If two people can't discuss their sex life, then it will be difficult to resolve it and find common ground.

When I work with a couple with physical intimacy issues, if the medical blood work checks out, then there is usually something deeper that has someone resist connecting sexually. As I mentioned before, there is a list of reasons why sex and physical intimacy may not be mutual. If sexual intimacy is an issue for you, here are a few recommendations:

- Don't make your partner wrong.
- Get to the heart of the issue together.
- Discuss *everything* from fears to fantasies.
- Negotiate until you reach common ground.
- Seek support if you need it.
- Let go of beating yourself up, feeling shame, and judging yourself or your partner if you are the one who wants sex less or more than your partner does.
- Create some fun together and try new things to see what can be mutual.

Emotional Intimacy

Emotional intimacy is perhaps the most important of the four types of intimacy. Connecting on an emotional level; sharing feelings, thoughts, fears, old wounds, goals and dreams; and allowing yourself to be vulnerable, sharing of yourself, while making sure you have a marital friendship, will help sustain the marriage. Imagine that one of you has surgery and can't be sexually intimate for 6-8 weeks during recovery. Then emotional intimacy and gentle touch will make a huge difference. Emotional intimacy can also include sharing loving words, saying "I love you," writing poems, giving cards with sweet words, expressing acknowledgment and appreciation, and complimenting each other. These words touch people at an emotional level.

Intellectual Intimacy

This level of intimacy is about talking, sharing, and discussing various topics. It can also include fun back-and-forth witty banter, witty being the operative emphasis. And it can include those deep and spiritual conversations. This level of intimacy brings a couple closer together because it lets them know they have interests in common they can discuss; shared interests can be a core value.

I once worked with a man who had been remarried for nineteen years. He cared about his wife and had two children with her, plus one child from a previous marriage. One of the children had a special needs diagnosis, but the difficulties associated with that were not a reason why he wanted a divorce. Instead, he felt he couldn't share intellectual conversations with his wife. He felt she wasn't that smart. I asked him whether in nineteen years she had taken some time to learn about the intellectual topics he wanted to discuss with her. He replied that she wasn't even capable because she was as dumb as a doornail.

On the inside, you can imagine what I was thinking as

a coach, but on the outside, I maintained my coaching poise and asked some follow-up questions. He was committed to improving this marriage, but he felt he had to look elsewhere to have stimulating intellectual conversations. His dream was to have that with his wife. He said other areas were going well, but if they didn't have a special needs child, he would divorce her in a minute due to their lack of intellectual connection.

So I say to all who are reading this book: Never underestimate the power of shared intellect. Choosing a partner who is at your intellectual level or who stretches you in one area while you stretch him or her in another only helps the marriage bond to grow stronger. If a big gap exists in this area, then there isn't the level of compatibility you had hoped for, and the marriage will likely succumb to the very high remarriage statistics, so if you are seeking a next marriage in your life, make sure there is a level of intellectual "we can talk about anything" kind of connection. If you already remarried someone and a wide intellectual gap exists between you, do your best to see how that gap can close. While no one wants to feel stupid, getting help from a professional can sort this issue out and hopefully help narrow that gap.

Spiritual Intimacy

For those who are spiritual, this intimacy level is powerful. Understanding something together and aligning in a shared belief in a power greater than yourself

> or the same religion can help build and sustain intimacy in the marriage. There is nothing like connecting through meditation, prayer, walking meditation through nature, or deep conversations about spiritual matters. Spiritual intimacy bonds you together as a couple, and in remarriage, the more levels of intimacy you have together, the stronger you are as a couple.
>
> For couples who don't feel they are spiritual, this kind of bond can happen in other ways. Sharing in your common love for something meaningful, or creating rituals and couples or family traditions together can also create a closer connection in a similar way.

These four areas of intimacy will truly ignite a close, solid, and sacred bond between you. Nurturing the intimacy as time goes on is critical, and opening up to be vulnerable is key. Intimacy is an area of marriage that is delicate to speak about, but as I mentioned earlier, communicating about it is so important. If you, as a couple, can't speak about it, then the likelihood of improvement isn't high.

I worked with a couple that had great intimacy at the beginning. They both found their sex life very mutually satisfying. They both had grown children and were raising one of the grandchildren. They created a rule that once sexual intimacy began, there were to be no interruptions. After a while, however, the husband's daughter started to text him, and he felt obligated to answer because he was trying to rebuild a better relationship with her. He started answering these texts during sex and would stop in the middle of it to read the text and respond. Needless to say, this didn't sit well with his wife; it made her not only resent him, but her stepdaughter as well. She felt that during sex was not an appropriate time to read a text, much less answer one, so it caused a lot of conflict until I had them create and commit to a new agreement during their together time.

Building trust and sacred intimacy in all four areas of intimacy is so critical to the marriage's success. Wholistic intimacy will allow intimacy to take place on a daily basis and keep the relationship vibrant, alive, and fun!

Exercise:

In the four areas of intimacy, where are we doing well?

____

____

____

____

____

____

In the four areas of intimacy, where do we need to make changes?

____

____

____

____

____

____

What can we do to take positive steps forward?

____
____
____
____
____
____

What do we want wholistic intimacy to look like for us?

____
____
____
____
____
____

Chapter 12

INGREDIENT 10—BLENDING YOU, ME, US, AND THEM

"I didn't give you the gift of life,
but the gift of life gave me you."

— Author Unknown

How complex can this topic get? Are you a remarried couple with no children? Did you know more and more remarried couples have no children when they remarry? Does that make every aspect of the marriage smoother sailing? Yes and no. While the marriage can be more focused on the nucleus (the married couple), there are still extended family members and potential issues to manage. You suddenly have old in-laws and new in-laws. Many remarried people still carry on a relationship with their former in-laws, and that is a complex issue for the new spouse unless he or she also still has connections with former in-laws—or isn't bothered by it. Some people want nothing to do with their former laws while some continue to see them. Now imagine this child-free couple having former in-laws, former step-in-laws, new in-laws, and new step-in-laws. We are talking parents, sometimes grandparents, siblings, cousins, aunts, uncles, etc.

Then there are people who maintain friendly connections to their former spouses. How does the new spouse feel about this? What is appropriate?

Then we have your new in-laws. Do they still have a connection with the former spouse? After all, for a while, everyone was family, but suddenly, when there is a divorce or death, that family bond changes. And what if your new mother-in law likes your spouse's ex more than you?

Can you see how complex this could all be, even without children in the picture?

So, if you are remarried or are remarrying, these are topics of discussion to have with your soon-to-be or new spouse. Where are the boundary lines? How can you follow the appropriate boundary lines as a team?

In my marriage, I am a stepdaughter on both sides of my family (mom and dad) since my parents divorced when I was nine and they have done very well in their second marriages. With those second marriages comes step-families, step-siblings, their spouses, their kids, my stepparents' siblings, cousins, etc.

I am close to a few and cordial with the rest. Rick's parents were divorced as well, and his father was remarried for over thirty years, but his stepmother passed away as did his own mom. Both women embraced me when I came into the picture, and while my family honestly would love Godzilla more than my former husband, they truly adore Rick. That said, we've all had issues regarding our in-laws, so we will explore how to cope with issues, both minor and severe, later in this chapter. On a positive note, being the nucleus of all of this extended family has been a very beautiful experience for us.

Then there are remarried couples who do not have children from their first marriage but are young enough to have them in this marriage. Being parents is a new experience for both of them. Having a child in this situation can be a very rewarding experience and create more focus on the nucleus and the new family they create together so that it almost feels like a first marriage. The couple may still carry issues from their previous marriages, but the bond they create as parents is uniquely theirs.

Now let's briefly think about how remarriage affects children. Children of all ages these days have parents, stepparents, siblings, step-siblings, grandparents, step-grandparents, etc. Imagine how big these families are for the kids! It was likely a challenge watching their parents' divorce, and now with a new stepparent and possible stepsiblings, life has really changed.

Blended families also come in many combinations. There are couples where each spouse brings children into the mix, and couples where one spouse brings children into the mix while the other spouse never had children. There are couples who both bring children in and then have one or two together, and couples where one has children and then they have more children with the second (or third) spouse.

So imagine being a stepdaughter or stepson, marrying someone else who is also a stepdaughter or stepson, and each of those people bringing children into the marriage and having more children together.

You seriously may need a flow chart just to sort out how everyone in the family is connected. I totally understand, and more importantly, there needs to be some organization, some boundaries, and some education about how family dynamics work, depending on the different blended family scenarios and which type you are.

These blended families can be lovely and fun, landing as a “bonus family,” but they can also be challenging, difficult, annoying, competitive for parents’ affection, and distant.

With so many factors to consider, the success of blending a family has to start with you, the nucleus or the couple.

If you have stepparents and/or former in-laws, it is important to establish agreements and boundaries. It is crucial that you and your spouse, as the nucleus, stay connected with each other on all fronts. It is the responsibility of the biological son or daughter, if they are adults, to deal with their parents and stepparents if there are any conflicts or issues. If the biological son or daughter are young children, the adults carry the responsibility for agreements and boundaries.

For example, let's look at a couple we'll call Damon and Melinda. They have been happily married for many years. Neither was married before, and when this story begins, they only had one daughter, Melissa, who was a toddler. Damon was the son of divorced and remarried parents. Damon and Melinda lived close enough to his father and stepmother that they were able to see them often. His father and stepmother formed a great relationship with Melissa, and she got to see them often. Damon's mother and stepfather would come to visit periodically, wanting to see them and little Melissa. The whole family would get together and go out to dinner since Damon's parents and stepparents were friendly with each other. However, when Damon's stepmother took little Melissa out of the restaurant following dinner and took a walk with her to spend alone time with her, Damon's mother became upset; she was only in town for a short while and wanted as much time with her little granddaughter as possible. It was tough because Melissa's step-grandmother spent a lot of time with her and was accustomed to it. But it seemed to Damon's mother that the step-grandmother was doing it on purpose, trying to establish her grandmother territory.

While Damon's mother was upset, she didn't want to confront her former husband's wife to request that she get more time with little Melissa.

Who had the responsibility of doing that? Damon. It was up to Damon as Melissa's biological parent to say something to his stepmother about it and to make sure his mother got the time she needed with her granddaughter. He did just that, his stepmother was understanding, and his mother got the time she needed.

When issues come up in blended families, it is recommended that the biological parent take the responsibility to handle the issue. If it is an issue with parents or a disciplinary issue with the parents' biological child, it is up to the biological parent to be the main disciplinarian. When children are with the parent and stepparent for a weekend or a week at their home, or if they live there with them, it then becomes the nucleus couple's home with the rules and boundaries set by that couple. The stepparent can do some disciplining at that point, but the biological parent must then reinforce his or her spouse and be the final word to his or her own children.

Parenting when stepparents are involved can be quite complex, but if the guidelines are set at the beginning, then the rules are clear and the kids will be less likely to act out.

They may, however, "act in." That is the other piece of that equation. Taking their anger, sadness, hurt, and frustration, and turning it inward is common, so it is important for parents and stepparents to make sure the kids are managing the situation from a psychological perspective, and that they know their biological parents are there for them. If they create a good relationship with their stepparent, that can be an added bonus.

Let's look at another example. Janet and Sam are newly married. It is Janet's second marriage but Sam's first. Janet had a young son, Mark, from her previous marriage. Mark had a difficult time accepting his new stepfather. His biological father wasn't easy to be with, so Mark was filled with resentment and hurt. Janet and Sam went on to have two of their own children together, so Mark felt like an outsider. It was up and down for Mark with his new siblings and his stepfather, but Janet and Sam were pro-active and did some very specific personal growth work so they had the skills to blend the family well. When Mark was old enough, he took the same personal growth program as his mother and stepfather did, and it brought all of them closer together.

Getting support or learning new skills and growing is often essential to make a blended family work well. Sometimes, it is even required for the couples with no kids just to deal with former in-laws and their own parents. Fortunately, being pro-active and doing a lot of personal growth work shifted their family dynamics, so today, they are doing well. The kids are all grown and they thrive together as a family.

Navigating Holidays

Holidays are one of the most challenging aspects of being a blended family. Whatever your spiritual orientation is, there will be holidays, birthdays, and special events such as graduations and weddings. It is very important that the co-parents/former spouses create a workable and cooperative schedule with the kids so they each get time with them during a holiday. That may mean having two Thanksgivings or two birthday celebrations. In my family of origin, we had Thursday Thanksgiving with Mom and Friday Thanksgiving with Dad. When they connected with their now spouses, we did the same. Holidays are important to learn to navigate so the kids involved feel loved, honored, and cared for. Having two Thanksgivings was a great thing for my brother and me, and my parents and stepparents collaborated harmoniously so our experience would be positive. Make it positive for you, your kids, and your step-kids. If you are a couple with no kids, you still have to navigate holidays and special events with new in-laws and possibly former in-laws whom you may still be friends with. You may have both parents and stepparents as well. Whatever your situation, remember also to honor the nucleus—you and your spouse—and decide together whether former in-laws are included, how you will navigate everything, and the degree of contact you will have with all of the family in your world. Then show respect to your spouse by not going against what the two of you have decided together.

Balancing Me and We

Regardless of the size of your family and/or stepfamily, you, again, are the nucleus of the marriage. It is, however, important to balance your time together and your time as individuals. Your time together is great quality bonding time, time just to be with each other, and time for adventures, fun, intimacy, vacations, nesting at home, etc. Your time as individuals is for your personal hobbies, your friendships, your career path, and whatever you need it to be within your marriage agreement, of course. Having space and time for yourself is just as important as having time together. In your previous marriage, you may not have understood why, at times, you wanted to be away from your partner, and perhaps he or she needed that time as well. That is perfectly normal. If things feel out of balance in either direction, then conversation and negotiation need to take place along with an inquiry to see whether anything is feeling off.

The bottom line:

- The nucleus couple is the first and foremost priority.
- Each partner is the final word with his or her own family of origin and stepparents.
- Each partner is the final word with his or her own biological children.
- The nucleus couple must come together as a team to set guidelines when any family is in their home.
- Each partner must do his or her best to create a positive relationship with his or her spouse's family and children.
- Each partner must maintain a co-parenting relationship with his or her former spouse if they have kids, or little to no connection at all if they don't, unless the current spouse is involved and in agreement.
- Guidelines are important when navigating all of this.

Exercise:

What is our new "family tree"? (Include biological family,

stepparents, and siblings, if you have them, biological children, stepchildren, and former spouses, if they need to be or are involved. You may want to use a separate piece of paper and draw a chart here.)

____
____
____
____
____
____
____

What are our guidelines with our families of origin as a nucleus couple?

____
____
____
____
____
____
____

What are our guidelines with our children and stepchildren (if applicable)?

____
____
____
____
____
____
____

How do we plan to enforce these guidelines as a couple?

What do we each need to do for ourselves as individuals?

Chapter 13

INGREDIENT 11—LIVING IN TRUST

"Few delights can equal the presence of one whom we trust utterly."

— George MacDonald

Do you find it easy to trust people, especially someone close to you like a new spouse? Yeah, me neither. In the last chapter, we talked about a few circumstances surrounding balancing in-laws and blended family issues. In this chapter, we will talk about trust, integrity, betrayal, and how a couple can build and rebuild trust in themselves and their marriage, even if their last marriage was full of lies.

Trust is a tricky thing because even the biggest liars and

cheaters will pitch a fit if they hear that they are not trusted. Most people on the planet have trust issues, whether it is a close loved one, a friend, family members, their boss, the government, and even God, if they are spiritual.

Humans just have a hard time trusting other humans. No one wants to be betrayed and feel that awful, sickening feeling that comes when betrayal happens. It is even an issue for those who say they have an easy time trusting others; they still keep an eye open. That's just human nature.

Trust and integrity also include guidelines for sharing private information. Yes, both of you have a past, whether you have been married before, engaged, or were just in a long-term relationship or two. It is not easy for your current spouse to hear about your past; however, it is a bonding experience to learn about each other through sharing. Here is a way to share in a mature and conscious way versus sharing gratuitously to make sure your partner is not jealous of your past because you choose to glorify it or you feel the need to brag. The deal is: it is your past, while your beloved is your present and future. Sharing intimate details about your past needs ground rules. Make them together and respect them together.

Another necessary point of trust in a relationship is to create ground rules about whom you share private information with about your relationship. Both partners should share with each other whom they plan to share with so the partner knows who has information. You can also decide whether there is information that is just off limits or only to be shared with a mutually-agreed-upon professional. It breaks trust to reveal private information to friends, coworkers, or family members that is not agreed upon by both of you. Family members are tricky because sharing when you have an issue with your partner can result in family gossip and being ostracized by your partner's family. We will define appropriate relationship-sharing agreements shortly in regards to this.

So let's start with some definitions. So many people forget to ask their partner what trust, honesty, and integrity means to him or her. They also often forget to ask what monogamy means to the partner, so it is common to think you are on the same wavelength with someone only to find out that your definitions are different.

If you are getting remarried, ask now. If you are already remarried, ask anyway.

Start with clarifying your own individual definition and what it would look like applied to a marriage. It is critical to clarify these meanings for yourself so you are clear when asking your beloved what his or her definitions are.

Honesty:

____

____

____

____

____

____

____

____

Integrity:

Trust:

Monogamy:

Lying:

Other Relationship Sharing Agreements:

____

____

____

____

____

____

Two people can say they have a core value of honesty, but have two different definitions of it. Two people can say they have monogamy as a deal breaker, but have two different definitions of what monogamy is.

I mention monogamy because if it is included or assumed to be included as part of the marital agreement, then infidelity is one of the worst types of betrayal someone can experience in a marriage. It is extremely difficult and painful to rebuild trust after that kind of betrayal. That's not to say it can't be done because several couples have done it, but it is incredibly challenging.

So clarify that you are on the same page with definitions first.

Next comes committing to and making an agreement about the guidelines and agreements in the marriage. Marriage can have a lot of freedom within it, but there has to be a container. Inside that container is freedom to be who you are, etc., but the container itself is the commitment, agreements, and guidelines you make to and with each other. When two people say, "I do" at their ceremony, they are making a commitment to the type of marriage they want. Hopefully, they have thoroughly explored what it is they both want (as explained in a previous chapter), have healed from the previous marriage, and have done enough inside-out work to be truly prepared to make this next marriage their forever marriage.

So commitment and guidelines are in place.

Now how do you apply these guidelines to stay on track?

It's very important to look at the previous chapter on letting go. If you don't start letting go of some of your own betrayals from your history as well as your moments of being the betrayer, then it is challenging to transform. Transformation, again, is an inside-out job. So go back to identifying old stories, beliefs, and patterns around trust, commitment, and integrity. Let go of old memories of what was or who you saw yourself as, and rebuild strength of character on the inside. Whom do you need to become in order to have this successful marriage? Whom you used to be is complete. It is in the past. You are a different version of yourself. You are an older, wiser version, so reevaluate whom you are, how you trust your own sense of self, and how you navigate your life. Look at what it takes to have that level of honesty, commitment, and integrity with yourself.

Then you can continue to work with your partner to apply the agreements made and the guidelines set.

What happens if an agreement is broken?

It depends on the agreement's level of value. If Tobias agreed to pick up some groceries for Beatrice on his way home from work, but he forgot, she might be annoyed, but she wouldn't end the marriage. If Tobias told Beatrice he was having some late nights at work and some dinners with clients from work, but she found out later that he was really having an affair with a coworker named Christina, that is infidelity, and infidelity for most people is a deal breaker.

What happens for a couple if their previous marriages ended because of infidelity or other deeper levels of betrayal?

That's a valid question, and a very tough one. So let's imagine another couple—Danny and Julia. In Danny's first marriage, he cheated on his wife and lied to her. Julia needs to hear Danny's side of the story in depth before marrying him. What led him to feeling it was okay to betray his first wife? What wounds was he carrying that were not healed that had him feel it was okay to cheat and lie? Or was it a marriage that wasn't really the best fit, but neither had the guts to tell the other? Whatever the reasons, Julia needs to know.

Can Danny explain his situation and his motivation to the degree that Julia can build enough trust with him to step into a marriage with him? Some would say, "Once a cheater, always a cheater," but infidelity happens for a lot of different reasons. Some people are just not built to be in a monogamous marriage. Some people just prefer the polyamorous lifestyle (more on that in a future chapter) because monogamy just doesn't work for them. Sometimes, people are just really afraid to open themselves to someone. Sometimes, the issues go back even further to their experience in their family of origin, which led to creating the experience in their first marriage. Our family of origin plays an important role in what we learn about relationships and marriage. This is our first understanding of relationships and marriage. As adults, we tend to duplicate what our parents did or do the exact opposite.

Learning the history of the person you are planning to marry—including his or her family experience, previous marriage, and other relationship experiences—will help guide you to make a decision about whether you can trust the person enough to marry him or her. An inquiry about the person's current intentions and how those have shifted from the past is also recommended.

Some people decide just to trust until they see evidence that they can't. Some people feel their trust needs to be earned, so they take things slowly while "testing" the other person to make sure he or she is trustworthy. The bottom line is you have to decide whether to move forward based on the information you have—although it can be considered an educated leap of faith.

As I mentioned previously, when my first husband and I were still dating, I saw red flags within the first month. Again, I was young and not very skilled in the relationship arena, so the red flags made me ready to end things, but I spoke to a counselor who encouraged me to stick it out and felt that I *should* (not a great way to make a decision) give the relationship a chance rather than be hasty. I was shocked to hear that, but I went with it. More odd things happened that weren't sitting well with me, and my intuition was right on the money. I found out he was seeing former girlfriends while claiming exclusivity with me. But being young and hopeful, I gave him another chance after breaking up with him for a couple of months. And he lied and cheated again. And I gave him yet another chance, and we ended up getting married. Did I prequalify him thoroughly? No. Did he earn my trust? No. Did I want to be married? Yes. I convinced him that this would work, that I was the right person for him, and I convinced myself that he would change.

So I was out of integrity with myself and living in a fantasy world with my hopeful expectations. During the marriage, his pattern of lying and cheating only continued and so did my hurt feelings. It was the ultimate betrayal of myself and my own instincts, and it really did a number on me. However, after that marriage, I was committed to learning and healing. I could have focused on what a louse my first husband was, but I chose to take ownership of my experience and realize that I was the common denominator since it had happened before. And I healed. And I raised my standards. Then I met my current husband Rick and the world of relationship and marriage completely transformed.

Healing from infidelity is deeply painful, whether you are on the receiving end or you are the one who cheated.

When going into a marriage with someone who has had either experience, it is necessary to know what kind of healing the person has done around that tendency, or that circumstance, because you don't want a repeat performance.

I could write an entire book about this topic, but I will just say to be cautious when going into a marriage with someone who has betrayed or been badly betrayed in a past marriage. He or she is likely to have wounds and issues from the experience, which is not in and of itself bad, but the person needs to commit to his or her own healing process in order for this next marriage to be successful.

Let me tell you the story of another woman I worked with where control and trust became issues in the marriage. For Nicole, it was her first marriage, but for her husband, Tom, it was his second.

Tom and Nicole were having issues and trying to decide whether to stay together. They had worked on some of their differences, but it was hard for Nicole to trust Tom because he felt the need to be in control. He made the money in the family, and they had decided she would be a stay-at-home mom to their little boy. Tom was a bit narcissistic and controlling while Nicole was more passive and didn't take a stand for her own needs. So Nicole was out of integrity with her own values, essentials, and must haves, feeling like if she walked away, Tom would try to destroy her and take their child away from her. Tom was a highly paid attorney so he knew ways to get around the law. Plus, he made the money and he made a lot of it.

Tom had also been verbally abusive with Nicole, and one day, he got physical. Nicole called the police while their two-year-old son screamed, but Tom didn't seem to care. The police came, but by the time they got to the house, things were calmer. So the police left and Nicole and Tom went on with life. But Nicole felt so betrayed by Tom's actions that she finally had the courage to walk away, and she did. Sadly, during the divorce, Tom was savvy enough to outsmart the court and take most of the money owed to Nicole. He also managed to get joint custody of their son. Nicole's life just wasn't the same after that. She felt even the court and her attorney didn't fight for her. She was exhausted from everything and focused on trying to put the pieces of her life back together. Eventually, she began dating and learning how to prequalify someone and learn to trust again. This time, her standards are different, and if she can let go of any kind of "rush" she feels to get remarried, then she is likely to do much better next time.

If people are trying to get remarried in a hurry because being divorced is scary and lonely for them, I say, "Slow your roll." Take the time. There is no rush. It is more important to prequalify and find a trustworthy person than to rush just so you have someone.

There are many other types of betrayals, and we will talk about one regarding money in a future chapter.

The ultimate betrayal is the betrayal of self; therefore, the more you heal your past experiences and build up trust in yourself, the more you are able to prequalify the right person to remarry. It's important to learn from the past, heal yourself, learn to trust yourself in a strong and powerful way, hold higher standards, and know your core values, core essentials, and deal breakers. It's also helpful to use your own intuition to tell you when something is not right.

If a second or third marriage has moments of deep betrayal, then it is not likely to be repaired without intervention, long-term help, major healing, and a long path to rebuilding trust. Betrayal in a second or third marriage is more difficult because of past marriage betrayals. If you choose to work things out, do everything you can, and know that some couples do make it to the other side, but the pattern is probably too deep to make a "quick" change. If you feel you can hang in there with your partner, then get some support from a relationship coach or some other expert to help you through the process of healing and reestablishing trust and integrity.

Friendships with the Opposite Sex

It is common these days for people to have several friends of the opposite sex. However, these relationships can bring up trust issues in the marriage, and again, guidelines and agreements need to be set between the two of you and then honored. It is helpful when you have a friendship with someone of the opposite sex to include your partner as much as possible. Allow your partner to get to know your friend. It is not always easy to build immediate trust, especially if infidelity and inappropriate behavior existed in a previous marriage.

Friendships with Former Spouses

Many people have actual real friendships with their former spouses. If you are divorced and single, it is much easier to be true friends with your former spouse. If you are remarried, however, the friendship can create trust issues. Again, guidelines are important, and understanding why you are friends with your former spouse is important to know. Including your current spouse in the friendship can help build trust in that friendship.

Reconciling vs. Repairing

From my point of view, when betrayal happens, specifically infidelity, there are two ways to go. One is reconciling. My definition of reconciling is different from others out there. For me, it is about coming to terms with what happened, why it might have happened, and the impact it had on both partners. It's about putting all cards on the table with complete honesty. Once everything is reconciled and on the table, there are two choices: 1) the couple can split up because a deal breaker happened, or 2) they can choose to move forward, get support, and repair the marriage.

Repair is about moving forward together to see whether the marriage can be recreated and the betrayal incident healed to the degree that the marriage can be fully repaired, evolve, and thrive.

Generally, there is more to repair than just the betrayal. Trust may have been weak in the partnership to start with. There may have been sketchy levels of honesty and communication already, as well as lack of connection and intimacy. The person who commits the betrayal is generally unhappy within him- or herself, feeling a lack of self-worth, a lack of appreciation from his or her spouse, and/or unhappy in the marriage in general, but he or she doesn't want the marriage to end or may be too afraid to step out of it. With infidelity, what draws a man in is visual attraction during a time when he is feeling what I just mentioned. With women, feeling heard, wanted, and cherished are three things that will draw her in to feeling attracted to a man. But when there are also internal stories, self-worth issues, and feelings of disconnection, she may feel she wants to end the marriage because it isn't working, while still being afraid to leave her spouse.

Whatever the contributing factors may be, getting to a point of repair is not easy. Repairing a marriage following infidelity or a betrayal of equal magnitude (for example, addiction of some kind, verbal or physical abuse, or spending large amounts of money without joint decision making) takes a lot of time and a lot of work. Can it be done? Sometimes. Is it easy and quick? No. There are two sides to the story, and I recommend a couple get some impartial support in order to move forward into repair mode. Specific steps need to be taken, and each person has to take ownership for his or her part, even if that part is an internal belief about him- or herself. That is incredibly challenging if the person is the one on the receiving end of betrayal.

So, in summary, building trust and integrity is about keeping your word and operating at the highest level of honesty possible, even when it's embarrassing or feels too vulnerable. This level of commitment is how the marriage bonds in a deeper way, and it is a big factor in contributing to the marriage's success.

Hopefully, your marriage is filled with honesty and integrity. As embarrassing as it can be and as vulnerable as it may feel to some, being honest is one of the main ingredients to creating everlasting love.

Exercise:

On a scale of 1-10, 10 being the best, 1 being the worst, how would you rate your overall level of honesty in your partnership?

In what areas of the relationship do you feel you haven't been completely honest?

In what areas of your relationship do you feel out of integrity?

In what areas of your life do you feel dishonest with yourself?

____
____
____
____
____
____
____
____

In what areas of your life are you out of integrity with yourself?

____
____
____
____
____
____
____
____
____

What do you feel you need to do to restore integrity and honesty with yourself?

____
____
____
____
____
____
____
____

What do you feel you need to do to restore honesty and integrity with your spouse?

____

____

____

____

____

What (if anything) needs to be reconciled in your marriage?

____

____

____

____

____

____

What (if anything) needs to be repaired in your marriage?

____

____

____

____

____

If anything needs to be reconciled or repaired, what is your plan to do so?

____

____

____

____

____

____

Chapter 14

INGREDIENT 12—MERGING YOUR $TUFF

"Money conversations are not sexy when merging hearts,
But there's no need to be greedy or grabby from the start,
When looking at all the decisions that need to be made,
Be conscious so they don't become a remarriage grenade."

— Author Unknown

How do you merge your stuff when moving in with your soon-to-be or new spouse? The process is quite different than it was the first time when you perhaps were not well-established in the world, right? In the last chapter, we talked about trust, and money is a big topic in the world of trust. In this chapter, we will look at the big merge of money and the many items you bring with you, the issues that can come up, and how this entire merge can actually flow well.

When you were married the first time, what did you actually have? What had you accomplished? What kind of money did you have? Most first marriages happen when we are younger, less established, and haven't accumulated a lot. Yes, some first marriages take place when people are older and already have accomplished things, have assets, etc., but this situation is most common in remarriage.

Think about it: You have been married before, so you have some items from that marriage, some mementos of it, especially if you had children with your former spouse. You also may have a career where you have accomplished things, and you may own a house, a nice car, dishes, etc., along with other financial assets. The question is: How do you merge everything with this next (and hopefully forever) spouse?

Some couples choose a prenuptial agreement. This is often seen as "Hey, we're planning on getting a divorce at some point, and I don't want him/her to get my stuff!" Or it can be seen as a way to make sure the biological children get something if the stepparent outlives the parent.

Prenuptial agreements can feel like a security blanket, especially if one partner has a lot more money than the other. They serve to protect money, homes, assets, or to control how things will be divided if the marriage doesn't work out. Do they reek of mistrust? Sometimes. Sometimes, however, good intentions lie behind a pre-nup. I recommend having an honest discussion with your prospective spouse if a prenup is in the picture. If it becomes clear that trust is the main issue behind the desire for one, that is a red flag and an issue you may need to work through before you decide to marry. You don't want to go into a marriage with someone who is expecting the marriage to fail from the start.

Other financial agreements are also necessary and good to have in place, such as a will and a living trust. It is also good to make clear decisions and agreements about how the bank accounts, stock portfolios, home titles, retirement accounts, etc., will be handled. Will everything be merged, or will each of you keep your own accounts and just jointly cover the bills? I always recommend a joint bank account and two individual ones, but I also recommend financial transparency.

If you both own homes, which home will you live in? Will you sell the other one? Will you sell both and just get a new home together? How will you handle who is paying for what? Will you be more traditional and allow the male in the marriage to be the main provider, or will you manage things jointly? These are important decisions to make.

How will you do your financial planning for the future, especially if children are involved? Will it be together as a couple and include the children, or will it stay separate?

If both people don't enter the marriage with many assets, it makes things easier financially. My former husband and I parted with each of us having a car in our own name and each of us taking half of our debt. We didn't own much, and I got the bulk of the furniture. We split the dishes, towels, etc. I got the bed and some friends donated their old one to him. We split things pretty fairly, but I also wanted some new towels, linens, etc., with new energy for the new chapter in my life that was beginning. I kept what I had until Rick and I bought new things after moving into a new home. He had been divorced longer than I had, and he had lived in a spiritual ashram for a while before I met him, so he had parted with many of his things. I met him about a year and a half after he left the ashram, so when we got married, we didn't have a lot of things that needed a pre-marital agreement. We discussed how we would manage our money together, and after a while, we purchased a new home, new furniture, and accumulated more financial assets together. Coming into this marriage without a lot of "things" made it easier to make decisions.

Whose furniture will you use in your home? What will you sell or give away? You both have dishes and blenders and linens. How do you merge your stuff?

The "stuff" part is a bit easier than the money. Some people don't want to part with something if it is a family heirloom, but as a couple merging, each bringing in a full set of living supplies, there is a point where some things need to be given away or sold in order not to crowd the home. It is hard if you want to keep your grandmother's dresser to remind you of her since she has passed on, but if you then have three dressers, something has to give. It is up to both of you to make those tough decisions when items are important but will crowd the home space. Having thorough discussions and staying in communication with sensitivity to your partner will help you both decide what stays and what needs to go. If your kids are grown and out on their own, things can be passed on to them, keeping them in the family.

Setting up the marital home can be a fun and exciting time, but it also requires some tough decision-making. Also know that sometimes you can set up your home and merge with things that are temporary, and then you can plan out a vision together of your ideal home and move toward that in smaller steps.

Merging also involves roles you will take on and contributions to the home and marriage you will make. These do not have to be gender-based roles. Honestly, if they were, I would be in hot water because a domestic goddess I am not. Some things will be gender-based, but my recommendation is to look at all that needs to be managed and divide the list according to who does what best and who likes to do what.

Here's another example from my marriage. Rick and I have two opposite style diets and eat different foods, so dinnertime for us means having different types of meals. Who is the better cook? Rick. I will share here that I have had a medical challenge that has made it more challenging for me to do certain things. I happily manage the money in our marriage and communicate transparently about what we have, what we spend, etc. I'm also the one to call the phone company, the cable company, the Internet company, and wait forever on hold to get technical support. Rick hates it. I don't love it, but I'm more open to taking that on. Rick handles the trash most of the time. (I do contribute there as well.) Neither of us have "fix it" skills, but Rick tries and can do certain things I can't. For cleaning, we both keep things up, but we have a housekeeping service come in biweekly to handle the heavier cleaning. We both do laundry; in fact, we will ask each other whether he or she needs anything thrown into the washing machine. We both get the cars washed, although Rick handles taking the cars in for service. So we really divide things up according to, again, who does what best and who likes to do it. Being the female, I am the one who spends more money, so it is only fitting that I manage it.

So, as a couple, go through the list of what needs to be managed and divide it up. That doesn't mean the other person can't chip in on a task taken on by his or her spouse, but it just makes life easier this way. If kids are involved, dividing up chores equally and fairly is the way to go, especially when there are two sets of kids. They all should have chores to do, depending on whether or not it is their primary home. Even if they are weekend visitors, there should be something for them to contribute.

Merging does not have to be a scary or challenging process. Once the financial issues are decided, the "stuff" is blended, and the rest is given away or sold, decide who is in charge of what, making sure that appreciation is expressed for what each of you is contributing, and making sure there is transparent communication and common ground negotiation if there is a disagreement.

Remarriage is an opportunity to create your new home and new lifestyle together. While there may be remnants of the past marriages, creating and managing your home and assets together and determining the flow and rhythm of your lifestyle is just another expression of the love and care you have for each other and for the marriage.

Have fun with this! Consult a professional such as a financial planner, a legal expert, or a tax accountant if you need support in that area. And, of course, hire a great coach if you want support taking these steps.

Exercise:
Use a spreadsheet for this exercise if you prefer.

Inventory of our current finances and accounts:

____

____

____

____

____

____

Inventory of our retirement assets, stock portfolios, and other assets:

____

____

____

____

____

____

Inventory of our monthly expenses:

____

____

____

____

____

Inventory of furniture and household items:

____
____
____
____
____
____

Action plan for our finances:

____
____
____
____
____
____

Action plan for how we will structure our accounts:

____
____
____
____
____
____

Action plan for merging our belongings (furniture, etc.):

____
____
____
____
____
____

Task list for managing our day-to-day finances:

____

Task list for managing our household:

____

______________'s responsibilities, contributions, and roles:

____

______________'s responsibilities, contributions, and roles:

____

The Kids (if applicable)

Assigned tasks and chores:

____

____

____

____

____

____

____

How we will handle things if there are conflicts in the area of merging and management:

____

____

____

____

____

____

____

Professionals we need to assist us with merging our stuff, money, with estate planning, or taxes:

____

____

____

____

____

____

____

How we will celebrate our success of managing our day-to-day life and responsibilities:

____

____

____

____

____

____

____

Have fun and get creative! Your household is now an expression of the two of you as a couple! This is part of your life together!

Chapter 15

INGREDIENT 13—GOING WITH THE FLOW

"For better, for worse, but never for granted."

— Author Unknown

Were you programmed as a child to believe that marriage is a fairy tale with a happily-ever-after? Did anyone ever teach you back then that many things happen in life that are not pleasant and often painful? Perhaps you already experienced some of that at a very young age or at other points in your life. You have already experienced pain through being divorced or widowed, and while your remarriage can be everything you dreamed of, every individual and couple will experience challenges, losses, grief, conflict, unexpected health issues, growth spurts, forks in the road, and other unexpected events throughout a lifetime. Most of you already know this from past experiences, but it's easy to forget to prepare for or at least expect the unexpected in the future as well. In the last chapter, we looked at some of the challenges of merging two lives together financially and how important it is to get on the same page because money is such a topic and fuel for conflict. In this chapter, we will look at managing the unexpected challenges that happen, and how you can turn to each other as a team to face them, rather than away from each other and end up in isolation.

When I coach clients, one of the common things I hear when working with single or single again people is that their vision does not include coping and managing the unexpected gracefully. Even people in their forties and fifties are saying they want someone super-fit with an amazing body, who is active, healthy, and financially well-off, and they would toss away someone who doesn't have those qualities.

I recommend being specific when it comes to envisioning your ideal partner, but I also encourage people to be realistic about the age stage they are in. While people in their forties and fifties can still be active, vibrant, and healthy for many years, it is unrealistic to think that nothing will ever happen to this "perfect, ideal" person you want to share your future with.

I will give you some examples.

I worked with a wonderful couple who was preparing to get married. She was very religious while he had served time in prison (not for murder). They both had some specifics for what they wanted in an ideal partner, yet they really fell in love with each other and were able to accept the other's history and appreciate the other's important qualities and interests. They both had very challenging histories as children with some abuse involved, for which they had both gotten help. She had been divorced once and also widowed, and she had two grown children and a grandson. Her beloved had been divorced, had two grown children, and was now a grandfather. Besides having been in prison for over a decade, he was also a war veteran who had suffered from PTSD. Those were not the issues they had about each other. What they needed to learn was how to manage the stories, programming, beliefs, and reactions they had to their own experiences and also how to cope with their partner having his or her own issues to manage.

I had such compassion for this couple, and I knew I could assist them despite the high level of challenges they had in their pasts that were seeping into their marriage and families. They had a complex situation, but they were really committed to being together and having a great marriage. They were willing to be vulnerable and transparent so we could manage not just the pieces of history that were coming up, but also the unexpected things involving their kids, grandkids, health, etc. These two were in their fifties when I first worked with them. They were in the premarital phase at that point, trying to look at how marriage would be, given all of the unexpected things that had happened to them, and how they could handle unexpected things in the future as just part of the flow of life. Once we worked on that, things moved forward for them and they got married.

After getting married, they ran into some challenges, so we

worked together again. Everything was worked out, and now when unexpected issues pop up, they practice the process I taught them to work through things swiftly. As a coach, I find it interesting that when a couple comes back to me, it's because they've often run into the same issues they had, but at a deeper level. In the world of coaching, it is important to practice the skills and clearing techniques learned so that things are cleared at the root level rather than just the surface. This couple still had some root issues harboring, so we just took a deeper cut with the same skills and techniques to make things better for them.

Issues, stories, limiting beliefs, and patterns usually have several layers, and often, we feel we have worked at the deepest layer we can in the moment, but then if a couple or an individual doesn't continue to work with them, the core level may not be reached and the conflict will pop up some more.

Even couples who work at a deeper root level still might get a bit triggered here and there, but they will know how to work things through because they learned the skills to do so.

Illness & Remarriage

As I mentioned before, it is unreasonable to expect that throughout several decades together, especially the latter decades of life, no one will ever get an illness. It is common for couples in their "golden years" to need hip replacements, knee replacements, or surgeries of some kind, and it is likely that at least someone will end up with some kind of physical issue or illness. It is sad when the illness is a heart condition, stroke, cancer, Parkinson's disease, or other devastating illness.

Speaking of illnesses, let me give you a person example. When I was eight years old, during a family camping trip (and I hated camping!), I was bitten by a tick. Back then, no one really knew that a tick bite could cause an illness. No information came out about tick-borne illnesses until four years later. I started having various health symptoms in my twenties, and by the time I was thirty-five, they were getting worse. I went from doctor to doctor, being misdiagnosed, until finally at age thirty-nine, I was diagnosed with Lyme disease. At that point, it was in its latter stage and hard to treat, with symptoms so painful I was mostly bed-bound. (My brain was and is fine, in case you are looking up Lyme disease on the Internet.) I didn't know much about it at the time, but now I have a lot of information, and my husband says I am a walking encyclopedia of knowledge. I'm grateful that I am doing much better.

My point in sharing this is that my health issues did not work for my first husband. We were younger and he wasn't up for dealing with any of it. He didn't realize that things like this could happen, even to people in their twenties, and he had little tolerance for it. The symptoms I had in my thirties were different and were getting worse. Most singles and divorced singles aren't looking for anyone with health issues. While it is everyone's right to visualize a healthy partner, it is unrealistic to think that the person you remarry will never have any health issues. It's unrealistic to think that you, yourself, won't either. Fortunately for me, my husband Rick loves me and chose me regardless. Rick is a spiritual counselor and a hospice chaplain, so he is trained to handle situations even more severe than mine. Neither of us knew what would lie ahead on that journey, but his love for me went far beyond what was happening to my body. He has been the most loving, supportive husband a girl could ask for.

Rick has also gone through his own health issues, and I have been there for him. None of these things are expected. Even when people knowingly remarry someone with a health challenge, they don't know where the path will lead.

No one knows what challenges lie ahead. Whether it's grief, loss, illness, or challenges with family, career, or children, the path of marriage isn't about having the "perfect" life with nothing to grow from. It's about bonding and learning how to handle those challenges; supporting one another; championing the other person; showing compassion, love, and understanding; and being the best listener and providing the most comfort possible. It is also an opportunity to learn to receive the same from your beloved.

Unfortunately, we grow up learning that challenges are often to be handled alone and that asking for help, support, or turning to a loved one is considered a weakness or character flaw. From my viewpoint, we are not having this human experience to be on "the island of me." We are here to connect to and love others, grow from challenges, and balance our giving and our receiving. It often takes more courage to receive than to give. It's in our nature, especially for women, to give, give, give, until we run out of fuel. For men, it is a natural instinct to protect and provide for others. To receive for a man, unless it is a paycheck, does not always come naturally. Receiving support, help, guidance, feedback, and even love from a partner is one of the gifts of being married. Giving and receiving is a dance, a balance; it is one thing to give or receive a gift on a birthday or holiday, and quite another to learn the balance of giving and receiving love and support. Marriage is one of the best opportunities to grow in that way, but during a first marriage, often that level of awareness just isn't there.

Imagine that as you grow older, one of you might have a heart attack, a stroke, cancer, or MS, or just changes in his or her appearance? Will you stop loving your spouse then? Will you give up on your marriage because of that? What if it happens while you are younger, much sooner than expected? Will either of you bolt?

The singles I work with may not be looking for anyone who has even a hint of a medical challenge, but once they get married, what will they do when something unexpected happens?

The following are some ways you can manage health situations in a marriage:

- Be kind and compassionate with the person going through the illness. He or she is likely experiencing a lot of pain, fear, loss, anger, and sadness. The last thing the person needs is judgment.
- Be helpful. The person's mobility may not be the same.
- Ask what you can do to support the person. Don't assume you know what he or she needs.

- Express reassurances, love, and your commitment to your partner regardless of what is going on.
- Take time for yourself. You need to recharge your batteries as well.
- Get outside emotional support to cope with what is happening. Life has suddenly changed, and it is not easy.
- Talk to each other about it. Turn toward each other.
- Allow yourself to feel the emotions coming up. The more you do, the easier it is to get to a place of acceptance about the situation.
- Allow yourself to receive from friends and family. Let people help. They may not know what to say or do, but tell them if they ask.
- Research information on the medical condition. Both of you need to be advocates. Doctors can only do so much. You are in charge of your own wellbeing.
- Understand that your social life may change. Learn to be okay with that. Your partner is the most important person in your life. Do your best to be the spouse and friend your partner needs.

These are helpful action steps to take when illness strikes. They can also be translated into action steps for other unexpected challenges and, hopefully, you can connect and love each other through it all.

Grief & Loss

Grief and loss are more common in second and third marriages because you are likely at the age stage where your relatives will pass away, a job might be lost, or kids will leave the nest. Grief and loss can look so many different ways and people go through so many different emotions. You may have already experienced grief and loss and have some ideas of what to do if you are the one grieving or if your spouse is.

Here is what you may expect for yourself or your spouse to experience:

- Sadness
- Anger
- Rage
- Depression
- Feeling "spaced out"
- Needing to be alone
- Needing to be active
- Needing to be connected
- Tears
- Fears
- Unpredictable states of being
- Waves of emotion

- Waves of being okay
- Sentimentality
- Wanting to talk about it
- Not wanting to talk about it or deal with it
- Stress
- Physical symptoms: aches and pains
- Not wanting to do anything
- Difficulty focusing
- Difficulty listening or being fully present
- Needing to sleep
- Inability to sleep
- Impulsive behavior
- Apathy
- Looking at your own mortality
- Wanting a drastic change in life
- Urgent motivation
- Needing escape through food
- Inability to eat much
- Fatigue
- Feelings of heaviness

- Yearning
- Numbness
- Feelings of emptiness
- Irritability
- Guilt
- Anxiety
- Vulnerability
- Abandonment
- Needing to withdraw from people
- Loneliness
- Wanting to avoid others
- Forgetfulness
- Slowed thinking
- Needing to retell the story of the loved one
- Annoyance with people who say inappropriate or triggering things
- Sensing the loved one's spiritual and energetic presence
- Dreaming of your loved one

The list can go on, but these are some of the more common things that can happen.

How can you be a good partner, or what can you do through your own grieving process to help get through the heavy part of the experience? Here are some tools you can use:

- Be patient with yourself or your spouse. The heavy aspect of the grief will go on as long as it does.
- Let go of asking, "Why?" The only answer is "because."
- Face the loss and help your partner to face it.
- Know that there are good days and bad days, and on a bad day, just accept that it's a bad day and it will pass.
- Know that you or your partner will get through this.
- Bring in something alive to care for such as a plant or pet. You may already have a pet. That can be helpful.
- Try and create a routine.
- Postpone major decision-making for a while. Decisions made on a whim from a place of grief aren't always the best.
- Try and eat regularly even if you don't feel like it or your spouse doesn't feel like it. The body needs the fuel.
- Be present to your needs or your spouse's as best you can.
- Listen.
- Share.

- Do not overdo activities. Let the body rest when it needs to.
- Know that grief is a natural process.
- Get support. Professionals can be very supportive and helpful.
- Ride the waves. The grief comes in waves and the symptoms come in waves. Ride them out.
- Be around people if that feels comforting.
- Be alone when necessary.
- Exercise or do some kind of movement. Keep your body healthy.
- Apply cold or heat to your body, whichever feels best.
- Do not compare your process with anyone else's.
- Be a good listener if your partner is the one grieving.
- Allow your partner (or yourself) the dignity of the process.
- Ask how you can support your partner. His or her needs can change from moment to moment.
- Ask for the support you need if it is your experience.
- Know that the grief will lighten more as time passes.
- Be with what is in any given moment.
- Allow the emotions to come forward. Let them out.

- Be present for your partner so he or she can let emotions out.
- Let people help. They mean well.

Losing a loved one will always feel bad, but grief will lighten over time, so be patient with your process or your spouse's process. There is nothing great to say about loss. We will all experience it. Knowing how to be there for your spouse is the best thing you can offer him or her, and allowing your spouse to be there for you is equally important.

It is a sad time when a loved one passes, so having this information can be helpful.

Loss of a job or a career change, a move, watching the kids leave the nest, or losing friendships are all different changes that can result in feelings of loss and grieving processes, but they aren't nearly as heavy as the loss of a loved one.

When illness, grief, or loss happens, as much as we try to fight what is in the moment, it only causes more suffering. Getting to the place where you can go with the flow, meaning be with what is happening, is the ultimate goal, even if that means tears, anger, feeling zoned out, or depressed. Those feelings will ease up at some point when we stop fighting them.

That doesn't mean that you don't work to take care of yourself, or that you don't get medical attention or psychological/emotional/coaching support during times of grief, but it does means a time of acceptance will arrive and you'll be able to get back in the flow of life, no matter how horrible what happened was.

Being in a lifelong partnership, even the second or third time around, means learning to manage the unexpected together. Turning toward each other for support and remaining connected is part of how you will make it through.

Chapter 16

REMARRYING OUTSIDE THE BOX

"Love recognizes no barriers. It jumps hurdles, leaps fences, and penetrates walls to arrive at its own unique destination full of hope."

— Maya Angelou

Growing up, were you taught about getting married, living in a beautiful home with a white picket fence, having 2.5 kids, good jobs, fancy cars, and fun vacations each year, and that was what was called marriage?

Of course, we know marriage is much more than that, but for some couples, a traditional marriage isn't their heart's desire. In the last chapter, we talked about going with the flow and understanding the ups and downs and the challenges that happen throughout the course of a marriage. In this chapter, we will look at some different types of marriages and even committed relationships. We will explore how couples can still create a great love inside of their own commitment containers, and we will look at some key guidelines that a committed partnership still requires.

Most of us have been through more than one committed relationship, and many of us through more than one marriage. A committed partnership can have a few different definitions to people, by which they do consider themselves "married." Let's look at a few different types of partnerships that may have been or felt like a marriage and had an ending, and now there is a new beginning or a newer partnership with someone else.

The Combo Couple

This couple is generally more traditional than some of the others I will discuss. In this couple, one partner was previously married and the other may have come close, been engaged, had a near miss or two, or lived with someone, but never quite made it to the altar. This combination couple may have some shared experiences, even though one partner never had a legal marriage and the other one did. While a relationship is a relationship in so many ways, a marriage takes it a step further. I have heard of and worked with people who have been a "committed" couple for so many years but just haven't chosen to get married. There are many reasons for that, which we will address. The combo couple may have had some similar and different experiences, but they have chosen to be together as husband and wife. Both partners may or may not have children, but being divorced is a very steep fall. Breakups from long-term relationships are painful, but different from divorce. The point is not to say that one suffered more than the other, but that one took on a stronger level of commitment than the other previously, and that person may have legal obligations with a former spouse that the other doesn't have. In my opinion, being married creates a different type of energy than living together or being in a committed relationship. That energy is hard to articulate. And when a couple is legally married, it is harder to leave. Marriage gives more incentive to try to work things through, and many steps must be taken before filing for divorce.

Combo couples can both bring past relationship experiences to the table. Some spouses in combo couple relationships who have not been previously married are choosing to be with someone who has the past legal obligations they personally have not had. Those past obligations might also provide reasons why it is impractical or even impossible for the couple to marry. The couple can see these situations as a challenge or an opportunity for growth and bonding; they are each other's spouses now or will be shortly, so they have to accept that dealing with child support or other legal issues from a past marriage is just part of the deal.

The "ingredients" for a successful marriage are still the same, but they may also include some blended family energy, along with more wounds, stories, or issues to release from the old marriage. Most people have dreams and plans when they get married the first time, but when the marriage ends in divorce, they have to let go of the dreams that will not be and start a new life for themselves. Breakups from any relationship can be painful, too, no doubt, but there is something unexplainable about the frequency or energy of a marriage compared to a committed relationship.

Here is a case in point: Patricia and Jeremiah are a happily married couple. For Jeremiah, this is his third marriage. For Patricia, it is her first. She had been engaged before, but it didn't work out. She has had several relationships, but never made it to the altar. With Jeremiah, she felt an instant attraction, and they both had the essentials and must haves each was looking for. Jeremiah had a daughter with his first wife, so Patricia became a stepmother, but she was young enough to still want children with Jeremiah, so they had a daughter together. They had some adjustments to make at the beginning of their marriage, but they have worked things through with support and are doing well as a couple and as a family. Patricia has learned what marriage is about, and Jeremiah has worked to clear the energy of his past marriages and get this one right! His commitment is strong, and they have created a loving family. Jeremiah's first daughter is older, so she is not in the home with them, but their shared daughter is a toddler, so they are raising her at home together.

Combo couples can have great marriages, and the spouse who hasn't been married before needs to accept the past and any connections he or she has with the former spouse due to kids or financial obligations. Everything else is all about how they choose to navigate their life together, and how they will learn and apply the skills and tools necessary to thrive in their marriage. The past marriage doesn't have to be an issue.

The "We'll Never Get Married But We Are Committed" Couple

With the very high divorce rates, many couples who have been previously married have become "gun shy" about taking the plunge into legal marriage again. They may commit to each other, live together as if they are married, and fall under common law marriage in some states, but they never actually choose to get legally married again. They may be perpetually engaged, making that level of commitment to live together, but not get married for financial reasons, while they would get married if the financial situation were different. They make a high level of commitment to their relationship, seeing it as a "marriage." Other couples are so afraid to get married again that they will live together as a committed couple, but their fear is so high that they will always keep open the option of leaving. These relationships don't always do as well because there is an easier way out, making the level of commitment weaker. The partners in this relationship don't always heal past marriage issues, and while they still need to learn, practice, and apply the necessary skills for a lifelong partnership, they may not choose to do so because of their fear. Some couples have this type of relationship because it provides a level of perceived freedom that they feel they need.

Again, all combo couples still need to make sure they communicate well; they must know that their values, core essential needs, and must haves are in alignment, and they need a vision for their life together. It is also helpful to have a commitment ceremony, whether legally based or not, to bring in the energy of a strong commitment. Such a ceremony solidifies the strong commitment, despite the reasons why you choose not to or cannot be married.

Polyamorous, Open Marriage, and Swinger Couples

Yes, some couples who remarry are interested in a polyamorous marriage or an open marriage. Other people who remarry choose to find a partner who wants to share in adventures as a "swinger" couple. The desire for an open marriage has to be mutual, and it may have been the reason for the previous divorce.

Even if people do want a polyamorous marriage—one where they are committed to each other and can also have romantic relationships with people outside of the marriage, which is mutually agreed upon—or have an open marriage—where they are open to seeing others as well—because they feel these lifestyles are what works for them, relationship skills are still needed. Communication needs to be effective and clear. Open marriage guidelines also need to be set so it is clear where the boundary lines are and how dating others will work. These couples still need the skills and tools to build intimacy, trust, integrity, honesty, and everything we have discussed to make their marriages work. Given that other people are involved, even the couples who choose to swap partners or "swing"—meaning having physical relationships with others and mostly swapping partners at planned events, which is mutually agreed upon by both—need to hone these relationship skills well and practice them carefully so their marriages can flow smoothly. They can create a vision for their marriage however they wish, so long as they agree to adhere to the guidelines they create together and use their skills and tools. The swinger, open marriage, and polyamorous communities out there that work do so because they operate inside a container of specific tools, skills, and guidelines so that the desire for the extra-marital activities are mutual and discussed. The container might be larger because others are involved, but agreements as to when they will have their dates with others, where the dates will happen, whether or not the spouse needs to meet the prospective partner—these topics all need to be discussed. Many of these couples who choose and resonate with these types of marriages are couples who are in groups of friends who are dating others in their group. Some people feel the need to know whom their spouse is with and even be in communication with that other person so they know their spouse is safe. The container consists of agreements and guidelines, like any other marriage, but their guidelines are different. The skills and tools they need are higher levels of trust, highly effective communication and conflict resolution skills, and agreements about privacy and sharing, just like a traditional couple would create. The container may consist of similar tools, techniques, and skills, but it may take more work to live this lifestyle. Jealousy may come up since it is part of human nature, even though they both feel they want this lifestyle. Many of these couples have children as well, so they need to decide how to present this situation to their children when they are older or whether they will share the information at all. It is not easy for polyamorous couples to feel safe enough to discuss their lifestyle outside of their community, and there are not many coaches and therapists who feel comfortable supporting these couples to work through their issues and create the marriage of their dreams. Interestingly enough, there are less instances of divorce for these couples because infidelity doesn't have the same definition as it does in a monogamous marriage. It happens when these couples hit a deal breaker, just like monogamous couples, but the deal breakers may be different.

An open marriage does not work if either partner is not 100 percent committed to the lifestyle or guidelines. As a coach, is not up to me to tell a couple what kind of marriage to have. It is up to me to look at the marriage the couple wants to have and help them create the proper container for it, so they feel the marriage is mutual and fulfilling.

Often, these couples in non-traditional but committed marriages and relationships have not been successful previously in a traditional marriage, but they finally found a better match in a partner who shares their vision for marriage or partnership. They often know better than I what is best for them given their situation, and again, my job is to help them navigate it.

Other people may feel threatened and not accept these types of couples. Just to be clear, it is very rare that anyone in a non-traditional marriage will "go after" or try to convert someone to their lifestyle who is happily married, or in the case of LGBT couples, who is straight. In my opinion, people are allowed to love whom they love so long as it is mutual and harmless. Rather than focus on judging or fearing other people's marriages, it's better to focus on your own. The more we focus on our own marriage and work on making it the best it can be, the more amazing it will be, and then our fears and concerns about what others are doing may, in fact, lighten up. While there are common skills and tools everyone needs for a successful marriage or partnership, not everyone is the same, and no one's marriage needs to be like anyone else's. It's yours and the two of you get to create it together.

One recommendation I have for non-traditional couples is to work on letting go of any *self*-judgments they may have. When you are in a non-traditional marriage that isn't well-accepted by society, it is easy to have internal challenges—self-judgments that can spill out into your partnership. Work on letting those go; get support if you need to.

Same-Sex Couples, Who Can Finally Get Married!

Because same-sex marriage was illegal until recently, little data exists on same-sex couples and remarriage. Many of these couples have been in long-term relationships and had commitment ceremonies and kids, and when the relationship ended, it felt just like a divorce. But now that same-sex couples can legally marry in many parts of the world, more statistics and data will come in and more information will be available to learn whether divorce and remarriage statistics are the same or there are any specific differences. That remains to be seen.

Exercises for couples in non-traditional marriages:

How we define our non-traditional relationship:

____

____

____

____

____

____

Our guidelines to create our relationship/marriage container:

____

____

____

____

____

____

How we create trust and intimacy in our lives together:

____

____

____

____

____

____

How we explain our relationship/marriage to others:

____

____

____

____

____

____

How we demonstrate our level of commitment to each other:

____

____

____

____

____

The challenges we have had:

____

____

____

____

____

____

Our plan to manage these and future challenges to keep our marriage/relationship on track:

____

____

____

____

____

____

Who we turn to for support when we are at an impasse or can't get through a challenge on our own:

____

____

____

____

____

How we manage parenting:

How we have been healing our past relationships or marriages:

What we want for our relationship/marriage moving forward, given its non-traditional circumstances:

For some of these answers, you can find recommendations in previous chapters. There is nothing wrong with your way of being in a relationship/marriage; it is just a matter of making sure that all is discussed, guidelines are set and agreed to, and everything is mutual.

Be happy. Create and live this marriage or relationship on your own terms, and do it as a team.

Chapter 17

INGREDIENT 14—KEEPING YOUR MARRIAGE ALIGNED

"Marriage is like a fine wine, if tended properly, it just gets better with age."

— Author Unknown

What was it that caused your first marriage to end in divorce? Marriages don't last for many reasons, and after what you have already been through, I know you do not want to be divorced or to break up with anyone again. So far, we have talked about living in truth and integrity; we have talked about keeping intimacy flowing in the marriage, and we have talked about effective communication. What else keeps a marriage aligned? Have you considered how much compatibility or what shared interests you have with your partner? Perhaps you didn't share much with your first spouse or you really weren't compatible. If there isn't the level of compatibility you thought or there is a lack of shared interests, then it is challenging to keep the marriage aligned. Without question, it's fine to have some differences, whether they are cultural, spiritual, or political (I'm not sure how political differences work, but they do for some people), and clearly there are gender-based differences, but if the gap is too wide with any difference, the marriage goes on life support, being too out of alignment.

Imagine that the marriage is a plant. (Just go with this….) And imagine that the plant needs nurturing, watering, and attention in order to survive. Surviving is great, and thriving is even better. Keeping up with day-to-day responsibilities with your head above water is also better than being upset and divorced, but keeping your marriage alive is also about making sure you add some fun, adventure, and shared interests into the mix, and you take the time to celebrate yourselves as a couple or even take a vacation or go out and have a nice dinner, just because. Don't let this marriage fall into a rut; make sure you have common interests and a strong level of compatibility. Don't let the marriage grow stale because then it will be tempting to stray or leave. It is not recommended to sweep issues under the rug or build up resentments toward your partner because you might be too afraid to rock the boat when you don't feel you are getting your needs met. Spend quality time together because the lack of it can damage the marriage.

Let's look at an example of why compatibility is so important. Jan and Bill are a "combo couple," except Bill had a child from a previous relationship. Jan had been married twice, and when she met Bill, it was under some out-of-the-ordinary circumstances, so she thought he was someone to pay attention to and he could be someone special. They dated briefly and quickly moved in together. Do I recommend that? Each couple is different, so it depends on the depth created between the two of them. I don't recommend moving in together as a way to "test the waters" because, as I mentioned before, for some couples, one foot is out the door, so there isn't a high level of commitment.

So Jan and Bill merged their lives together and Bill's daughter, Madison (age five at the time), spent time at Bill and Jan's house on weekends. For some reason, Bill chose to keep Jan and Madison separate in his life. When Madison visited their household, Bill would even choose to sleep in *her* room and not return to the marital bedroom to be with Jan. Bill and Jan did spend some time together, and Bill, who didn't have a full-time job, would cook dinner for Jan when she came home from her busy corporate job, and then he would leave to spend time alone or spend time with Madison during the times she stayed with them. Intimacy was lacking in this marriage, so the marriage was barely surviving, much less thriving. There was a lack of conscious communication on Bill's part, and a lot of upset feelings for both of them, especially for Jan, who felt edged out, unappreciated, unloved, and uninvited. Bill would create activities to do with Madison, with or without Jan. Bill and Jan seemed to have little compatibility, and there was little attempt on Bill's part to look at shared interests and be attentive to and communicative with Jan.

After a while, even with all of the effort Jan put into the partnership, there wasn't much that was keeping this marriage aligned. Jan wasn't seeing much of Bill, which was Bill's choice. Jan was asked to stay away when Madison was visiting, even when Madison got older, and even though Jan was trying to develop a relationship with her. And Bill wasn't even close to being a financial provider, so Jan felt she was paying for any adventure or special occasion they had or might want to have. Keeping a marriage aligned is mostly about compatibility and shared interests, but it is also about the other areas as well. Letting the marriage go on life support practically guarantees that one or both spouses will eventually pull the plug. In this case, Bill allowed that to happen.

Eventually, Jan felt like not only was she being edged out, cast aside, and unloved, but the marriage held little fun, was hardly an adventure, and she was in charge of everything. Jan felt like she and Bill were leading separate lives with little connection and shared interests. It is hard to keep a marriage aligned when one person isn't willing to spend special quality time with the other, or withdrawing from his or her spouse. Bill was not watering the relationship "plant," so it wilted and eventually died. Jan finally asked for a divorce, feeling like the marriage not only lacked fun, alignment, and vibrancy, but also the very basics. Bill let go and allowed the marriage to go on life support, and as much as Jan tried to revive it, she finally felt she had to pull the plug.

Making special moments in a marriage is quite important. Making it more than just day-to-day survival, or a duty and responsibility, takes the marriage to a whole new level. Making it special each and every day creates not only alignment, but aliveness as well.

Sharing Alignment

Again, one of the most important aspects to keeping your marriage aligned is sharing interests and being in synchronicity through compatibility, so you can have fun, "get" each other, be adventurous, and philosophize and spiritualize in a way that suits both of you and allows quality time together. If keeping the marriage aligned means two different things to two different people and lacks shared interests and time needed together, the marriage is going to be on life support because two people leading separate lives isn't going to work for most couples.

Another couple, Carolina and Craig, were both in a second marriage. Carolina loved nesting in her beautiful home and finding fun and adventure at home. Craig, however, was an adventure guy, a thrill seeker. His idea of alignment was for them to ride his motorcycle, fly airplanes, go to boxing matches, visit amusement parks, go sailing, and go on road trips. Carolina's idea of alignment was having a stimulating and spiritual conversation, cuddling up to the fire while watching a good movie and sharing a good meal, taking romantic walks, engaging in deep spiritual practices together, going out to eat, learning new things, going for massages together, visiting bookstores, and really being able to share with each other. She had little interest in Craig's adventurous, thrill-seeking nature, but she thought he would change in the marriage. He acted like he would for a while and pretended to be interested in similar things, but soon, Craig was paying little attention to Carolina and her interests. He was self-centered and figured once he had done the wooing, he could go back to his interests and she would follow.

The marriage ended up on life support. Craig rarely wanted to talk and be with Carolina. He would just take off when it suited him to go on an adventure, leaving Carolina home alone. In short, he didn't nurture the relationship or water his side of the marriage's "plant" because he expected Carolina to do it for him. His idea of alignment was doing things his way, and if Carolina didn't want to join him, he would just go anyway. He didn't seem to put effort into keeping the marriage aligned and vibrant, or even in survival mode, so Carolina filed for divorce and pulled the plug.

Keeping a marriage aligned is about so many things, but shared interests and true compatibility often get underrated and passed over, initially because the chemistry and some other things seem so amazing.

Since you're reading this book, you have likely been married before. Outside of your former spouse dying, your former marriage probably either had infidelity or betrayal, or it lacked compatibility and shared interests, leaving it in a rut. It may have gotten caught up in the day-to-day survival, so it didn't get the proper vibrancy, nurturing, and aliveness that it required to go the distance and be fully aligned.

This time around, it is important to make sure those pieces are in place.

Exercises:

Where we are truly compatible:

Where we have differences in our likes, dislikes, and ways of being:

Shared interests/activities we both like to do together:

Interests/activities we don't share:

How we balance the differences:

How we keep our marriage aligned:

Chapter 18

INGREDIENT 15—LIVING CONTENTLY-EVER-AFTER

"Marriage is like watching the color of leaves in the fall; ever changing and more stunningly beautiful with each passing day."

— Fawn Weaver

I know you have heard the fairy tale concept of happily-ever-after. That was programmed into the fairy tale fantasy idea of what marriage is. Since most of you have been married before, you know happily-ever-after isn't anything that can be sustained in a marriage. From my viewpoint, it can only be internally sustained and to a certain degree. Contentment is a balance of the highs and lows, and while the highs in marriage are exciting, the lows are disheartening. While the lows can mostly be repaired, we cannot hold on to the high moments, so the bliss in marriage is about being in a state of positive contentment.

A difference exists between being content vs. being in a place where you feel you just have to endure "what is." Marriage is not a commitment to tolerating or enduring anything. Yes, there may be moments of having to endure a movie the other one wants to see but you don't, or enduring seeing your in-laws, or doing an activity that pleases your partner but not so much you, but marriage is not about a lifetime of just tolerating being married. Positive contentment is about being pleasantly content about your marriage overall. Marriage will always provide opportunities for learning and growth, which we will talk about in a bit, but knowing you are pleasantly content, with moments of extreme happiness and some crappy unfortunate lows, will help the marriage be successful over the long-haul.

Evolution

Like anything else, marriage evolves and goes through growth spurts, and the two people in it evolve and grow as well. When two people are committed to personal, spiritual, and marital growth, the marriage gets better, deepens, and opens to more expansive love and experiences. Individual growth is critical to our lives in general, and marital growth is critical to its success.

If you examine your own life now, are you the same version of yourself as you were at age eighteen, or twenty-one, or thirty? Of course not. It is true that the essence of who we are does remain, but so much of us changes and evolves over our lifetime that our marriage needs to grow as well.

Here is a list of the common areas where growth happens and needs to happen:

- Belief systems
- Core values
- Core essentials
- Career path
- Communication tendencies
- Levels of affection
- Trust
- Honesty
- Spirituality
- Self-awareness
- Awareness of others
- Awareness of the world
- Likes
- Dislikes
- Vulnerability
- Routines

- Rituals
- Self-care
- Reactivity
- Connection
- Geographical location
- Communities
- Friendships
- Areas that cause life-altering challenges
- Level of commitment
- Wisdom
- Appearance
- Goals
- And many more

In whatever area you feel you need to grow or you are changing, it is important to stay in open and honest communication with your partner about your individual internal shifts and share how you are evolving as a person, as well as any changes that directly or indirectly could affect the marriage.

It is also a sign of mindfulness, good communication, and intimacy to share with your partner. It is even more fun to make a commitment to grow together in certain areas, whether it means learning something new, going to a new spiritual community together, trying a new activity together, or visualizing together for a common goal.

If the gap of growth and development gets too wide, it is challenging for the marriage to continue working. Staying in communication and in the spirit of growth will help keep the marriage on a good and positive path that will allow you both to bond even further.

Using challenges as an opportunity for personal growth

From my point of view, every experience we have is an opportunity for personal growth, evolution, and awareness.

Imagine that life is like one big university curriculum. You have your goals (your major and minor). You have your difficult past (your undergraduate and graduate curriculum), and you have homework, exams, a need to study, and the completion of the parts of the curriculum. If you were an ambitious soul, you may have decided to double major and take on a more challenging curriculum. Being married more than once indicates a heavier curriculum in the area of relationships. Why is it that way? It's just what your soul took on as an area for major growth, transformation, and deep change. It appears that we, in our human experience, don't choose those more challenging areas, but from a soul perspective, in my opinion, we do. If marriage is the curriculum area we took on for the most growth and evolution, then it is important to make it about you rather than the "horrible people" you have chosen previously. It is important to take full ownership of your experience and just go with it as a challenge to see how much you can grow and evolve. However you respond to the issues that come up, your "curriculum" is, in fact, the real issues wanting to be released and healed. That is where growth often happens. It happens by being aware of what triggers us and what disturbs us. Pay attention to those triggers. Make it a team effort with your partner who has his or her own curriculum, but given that this is likely a second or even third marriage for you both, there is a need for a higher level of mindfulness, learning, and vigilance in this area of life.

Have you ever noticed how easy marriage and relationships seem to be for some people? That is because it's not their primary area for tough curriculum. It is still part of their life curriculum, but they may not need upper division courses or their courses may be simple for them. The minute we compare our life curriculum to that of someone else, we will start feeling bad about ourselves, so it is not a useful thing to do. Another thing that people tend to do that is also not useful is to compare where they are with where they expected to be at their age. While we all have an expiration date in this human experience, getting caught up in "where I thought I would be at my age" only leads to being upset and suffering. Letting go of those tendencies is helpful and removes blocks from your path forward.

For an example, let's look at a remarried couple who got caught up in comparison. Tia and Henry have been married for about six years. They love and adore each other, have a great marriage, great careers, great health, a beautiful home, loving families of origin, and earn good money. All areas of their lives seem to be on track, except that they want to have a baby together and, for some reason, haven't been able to. Being in their late thirties certainly makes conceiving more challenging, and neither had children in his or her previous marriage. While they have lots of nieces and nephews, having a baby of their own has been a must have for both of them. Many of their friends and neighbors have been getting pregnant and having babies so easily that it has been painful for this couple to watch, as happy as they are for their friends and neighbors. Comparing themselves to the others, which is hard to do when it is a bit in your face, is not helpful. It has only made them feel bad, made it hard for Tia to go to baby showers, and has brought them both a lot of sadness. If they can stay focused on being parents with an open heart for adoption, and trust that it will happen either way, then they will find it easier to be around the children of their friends, family, and neighbors.

Fortunately, Tia and Henry were able to see what they were doing to themselves and refocus their energy. They learned how to work through any upsets that came forward, realizing it wasn't as much about seeing babies and having a challenge becoming parents, as about judging themselves. Self-judgment can be painful and slow our growth until we learn to forgive ourselves and let go of it.

Painful experiences can happen, but suffering over them is optional. Using the techniques I presented earlier can really help release those self-judgments and negative comparisons; once released, it will open the flow of moving closer to your goal with more grace and more ease, even if it is an "upper division" course in your life curriculum.

Here is another example of a couple I worked with who was in their second marriage. Sharon and Conrad had children together, and he had children from his first marriage. They had learned a lot from their first marriage experiences and were both committed to personal and spiritual growth and liked doing activities to promote that growth together. At one point, Conrad felt he needed to speed up his growth; soon, he was moving fast in his areas of interest to the point of exhaustion. He started to judge Sharon because she was not speeding up with him. She was growing at her own pace because it was a pace that worked for her since she also had her own business and home schooled the younger children. Conrad's issue when they came to me was that he was on a fast pace with his growth and he was not happy that Sharon was staying at her own authentic pace. Through coaching, we discovered that he had issues underneath his reason for wanting an accelerated growth pace that had nothing to do with Sharon and everything to do with his family of origin. When I asked him what he thought he was racing toward, he really didn't know. Was there some kind of place called "Enlightenment" he thought he could get to? Through our coaching process, Conrad realized how hard he was being on himself and on Sharon, and he decided he was not in a hurry. While his growth remained important to him in his life and marriage, he knew slowing down needed to happen because his pace was starting to affect his health and his marriage.

This couple used this difficult experience as a means for personal growth. Because deep communication had been replaced with judgment, they realized together that they needed to communicate more about their fears and "aha" moments of awareness so they could remain in synchronicity. Conrad learned he needed to be more vulnerable when sharing with Sharon, and he learned he needed to let go of some of his self-judgments and limiting beliefs.

So take everything that feels challenging in your marriage. Pick one issue to see as a HUGE opportunity for learning. Notice what comes forward and let it give you the opportunity to squeeze up the reaction, the limiting belief, the self-judgments, the stories, and the early programming still living inside of you. Then notice what you have learned. Notice what you are experiencing in this marriage and see how you can grow from it. Lack of compatibility and deal breakers are still opportunities for learning, but they don't mean you have to stay in the marriage with that person.

Here's one more second marriage example. Jim and Olivia had a rocky start but created a good marriage. Things went smoothly for many years, along with a few of the usual conflicts, until Olivia noticed a file on their computer. When she opened it, she realized Jim had been indulging in porn, collecting photos of sexy, scantily clad women; even worse, he had a mistress and had put himself on several dating sites. Olivia was so devastated that she started to consider divorce and an exit strategy. After she confronted Jim, she learned that Jim had a sex addiction and needed help for it. He so badly wanted Olivia to stay with him as he healed from his addiction. As hurt as she was, Olivia entertained the idea, but ultimately, she felt she couldn't do it. She had to honor her must haves/deal breakers and go her separate way. She asked for a divorce and moved out, and they both moved on.

This was a tough situation because as much as Jim wanted the marriage to stay intact while he went through his healing process, Olivia just felt she couldn't do it. Olivia had a choice to make, and she made a choice that she felt honored her "must have" list. So as challenging as it was for her with her "curriculum" in the area of relationships, she was determined to heal and learn from the experience, but it didn't mean that she had to stay in the marriage in order to learn, grow, and evolve.

It is important to take life and marriage's challenges and do your best to see them as part of your life and marriage curriculum, as well as opportunities for growth and evolution. It is also critical to keep up your own intentions to grow and learn so you can continue to evolve and your marriage can deepen. Don't let the gap grow too far apart—grow together!

Exercise:

1) What is coming forward for me as an individual that is calling me to heal, grow, and evolve?

____

____

____

____

____

____

____

____

____

____

2) What am I doing to grow?

3) What is coming up for us as a couple?

4) How are we growing as a couple?

5) What are we doing to evolve intentionally and become more self-aware and more self-realized?

Keep working through these exercises, and when you identify what is trying to come forward for healing and growth, look at the different options for working with them. Continue to reach toward a level of contentment within yourself, your life, and with each other. Life and marital harmony is a beautiful thing.

A Final Note

KEEPING UP WITH THE JONESES

"The most splendid achievement of all is the constant striving to surpass yourself and to be worthy of your own approval."

— Denis Waitley

We've all heard the term "keeping up with the Joneses." It means trying to keep up with neighbors, friends, and other couples in a material way that results from feeling a need for others' approval. It can even mean wanting to feel better about your own circumstances because hearing what everyone else is doing or achieving in their marriage or family can trigger personal feelings of unworthiness, envy, and frustration. In our last two chapters, we spoke about keeping this marriage aligned and living contently-ever-after. This can go awry if we are constantly trying to live up to the standards of others. In this last chapter, I'll use the term to mean keeping up with your *own* marriage—your *own* progress as a couple—and implementing the practices in this book that you need. Your own approval is the only approval you ever need. Take your marriage and your life at your own pace. Do what you both want to do for yourselves, and have the marriage that you want to have (as long as it is mutual and harmless). The rest of the world's approval is not required. Keeping up with anyone else's way of life is not necessarily even healthy for yours.

Throughout this book, we have explored many ingredients of what makes a remarriage successful, as well as information that creates awareness about what can harm it. While much of this information can be applied to *any* marriage, a difference exists between a first marriage and a remarriage, and much of that has been differentiated here. We have looked at myths and challenges, the ten phases of a relationship, and increasing awareness by being in the know. We have explored core values, core essentials, must haves, deal breakers, talking points that result in communication pitfalls, and talking points to improve your communication beyond the cliché. We have discovered how to play nice by learning better ways to resolve conflict. We have learned to let go of the past with some technique recommendations. We have explored increasing your connection through wholistic intimacy, blending families while balancing yourselves as a couple, living in truth through deeper honesty and integrity, and merging your stuff and dealing with money as a remarried couple. We have found ways to handle the ebb and flow of challenging and painful situations that happen over the course of a long-term marriage, and we have learned how to go with the flow. We have looked at non-traditional couples and how they may have insight for keeping a marriage flowing well, and we have looked at what it means to live contently as you embrace individual and marital growth.

Putting all of the ingredients together, taking note of the information, and acting on my recommendations takes time, consistency, practice, and commitment. Keeping up with the Joneses (That would be you!) is not automatic or always easy to do, but one phase of a relationship is *mindfulness*, and it is an ingredient that must be happening all the time. It is important to "take the temperature" of the marriage, check in with each other as a couple, and share what is happening, where you both are, along with your goals and dreams for the future. Dare to dream for yourselves individually and as a couple.

Keep up with your own vision of your future together through visualization. Visualizing and navigating your life together can be done in several ways. You can create a cork-board vision board together by cutting out magazine pictures of the future you want to have with words cut out or written to describe that future. If you create a vision board, use push pins so you can easily move or remove items because some aspects of your vision will change. If you are more into a narrative, write a vision for your future in the present tense, such as: "We are enjoying the trip in our new sailboat." Write it as a story as if it is happening now. Keep up with the flow of conscious creation together as individuals and as a couple.

That is such an important aspect of flowing in harmony, in excitement, and in adventure together. You can add to the vision board or narrative how well you are doing with these relationship skills, how graceful your communication flows, how beautiful your new home is, how much you love your new job, how easy and fun it is to have a blended family, and how much your new in-laws love you.

Make this vision fun, filled with the desires of your two hearts, and know that it reflects where your marriage is going. It is another great bonding exercise.

I also recommend you hire a coach like me. Coaching is not just about getting help to move through conflict or challenges; it is also about working on these skills, keeping your marriage reenergized, discovering ways to increase intimacy and connection, and moving through challenging circumstances. Having regular couple check-in sessions to see where things are and what you want to focus more on together, or to be pro-active rather than reactive, is another way relationship coaching can help. Group programs can help as well.

I believe marriages flow best when there is a conscious effort to keep everything on track, be proactive, create a vision together to help you navigate the marriage forward, and of course, when you keep evolving and healing the past.

I offer private coaching for singles and couples as well as virtual classes that focus on the areas I speak about in this book. I also offer home study online programs to continue the flow on your own. (See the coaching page at the end of this book.)

It is my great joy and passion to see a marriage thrive, especially if it is a second or third marriage and the partners have each finally found the truest mate for their souls. I believe marriage is its own entity and needs time, love, and attention. Again, imagine your marriage as a plant that needs both of you to water it, to tend to its soil, and to give it fertilizer and sunshine in order for it to stay healthy and continue growing. Keep tending to and nurturing your marriage. By practicing your marriage skills, you will be able to watch it grow and bloom. By integrating these ingredients, you can create the perfect marriage cake! I challenge you to write 10 action steps that you are willing to take after reading this book to truly integrate the ingredients, the skills, the tools, and what you are taking away.

1. ______________________________

2. ______________________________

3. ______________________________

4. ______________________________

5. ______________________________

6. ______________________________

7. ______________________________

8. ______________________________

9. ______________________________

10. ______________________________

Thank you from my heart to yours for reading this book and not throwing in the matrimony towel. Marriage is a true gift—one to be treasured and cherished. If you need further help, I can be contacted through my websites: www.RemarryingRight.com and www.ConsciousSoulMates.com. You can even contact me through my private number to discuss getting the support you need: 818-232-3186. It would be my privilege to support you in enjoying the blessings of a beautiful marriage together that finally lasts a lifetime. I wish you an amazing journey on your path to Remarrying Right.

"Love is the greatest gift when given.
It is the highest honor when received."

— Fawn Weaver

Treat yours consciously,
tenderly, gracefully, and graciously….

About the Author

SUSAN ORTOLANO, M.A, PCC

Susan Ortolano, M.A., PCC is an Intuitive Relationship and Marriage Coach, Best-Selling Author, and Professional Speaker. As an International Coach Federation (ICF) Professional Certified Coach, she has also been a Relationship Coach trainer for international coach training academies.

In addition to her global coaching business, Susan also works as a Clairvoyant & Medical Intuitive, providing intuitive readings for her global clientele.

Susan has taught and trained many Relationship Coaches around the world, and she has a passion for helping singles and couples learn the tools and skills to live their own great love stories. She loves sharing how to master the art of successful relationships. She was partially inspired to help others in relationships and marriage by her own personal journey of having challenging relationships, leading to a painful first marriage, and finally understanding what she needed in order have an amazing second (and forever) marriage, with her husband Rick.

Susan started her career as a multiple award-winning high school Spanish and Life Skills teacher, with students flocking to her for advice about their teen romances—that was when she first knew she ultimately wanted to help people find lasting love.

Teaching, coaching, speaking about relationships and marriage, along with using her intuitive gifts are Susan's great joys. In her spare time, she and her husband Rick love spending time together. They enjoy dining out, binge-watching TV shows and movies, reading books, and studying many aspects of spirituality and intuition. With several academic degrees and certifications, they both have a zest for learning, personal growth, helping others, and love nesting in their beautiful home surrounded by the mountain canyons north of Los Angeles, California. Visit Susan at:

www.ConsciousSoulMates.com
www.RemarryingRight.com
www.RadiantPathways.com

UPCOMING TITLES BY SUSAN ORTOLANO

Premarrying Right

Are you engaged and about to take "the plunge" into marriage? You may be planning your dream wedding but are you planning your dream marriage? Most couples don't know that the transition from engagement to getting married to becoming newlyweds is a process that most are not prepared for. In this book you will learn the skills and tools couples need to make that transition a smooth one and acquire the right skills and tools to adjust to married life together following the engagement and wedding. Readers will also learn the ingredients for building the foundation for a fantastic marriage that lasts. Getting married and starting a new life together as newlyweds can bring forward many obstacles, old patterns, deeply stored issues from the past, along with unmet expectations that couples are not expecting, even if they have been living together. *Premarrying Righ*t helps readers plan and prepare for their special day along with a graceful and easy transition into beginning a marriage and helps navigate a powerful path for their future together. Exercises are included.

Manifesting Mr. Right

Are you single, female, and in your midlife years, wondering why the heck you haven't found the right guy? In this book, you will learn how to become "relationship ready." Many women think and feel they are ready for marriage, only to continue to attract the wrong partners. This book helps readers get their own inner and outer "house" in order so they can be free from the blocks that have been unconsciously standing in the way of their relationship goals and dreams, learn some of the dating pitfalls that so many women find themselves in, and learn how to be, energetically and realistically, an invitation for your true love to find you while learning how to be the love that they already are. Step-by-step actions and exercises are included.

Keeping Marriage Right

Is there a "right" way to go with the flow of the unexpected challenges of marriage? This book is about the unconditional love required to keep your marriage and other types of relationships strong through chronic illness, terminal illness, life-altering injury, and other challenging circumstances that no one wants to or expects to experience. How do you cope if it is happening to you? How do you manage when something is happening to your spouse, your best friend, your parent, your sibling, or anyone close to you? This book teaches couples how to manage these unthinkable and painful situations with grace, continued connection, intimacy, self-forgiveness, self-care, compassion, and love. Marriages and relationships with these circumstances can still continue to grow, evolve, and thrive. This book lights the way to that process of keeping marriage right in the face of the unexpected challenges. On a personal note, it is inspired by my own experience living and loving with Lyme Disease, watching my mother and stepfather live and love through four types of cancer, and watching others live and love through physical, financial, and medical adversity. Just when people who are ill, struggling, or injured think no one will ever love them as they are, they learn through this book what loving unconditionally and keeping marriage right truly is.

For release dates and the latest information about Susan Ortolano's books, visit: www.ConsciousSoulMates.com

About Relationship and Marriage Coaching with Susan Ortolano

LEARNING FINALLY TO MASTER THE ART OF SUCCESSFUL RELATIONSHIPS!

As an Intuitive Relationship and Marriage Coach, Susan Ortolano, M.A., PCC uses her gifts as a professional clairvoyant and her extensive coach training to help singles manifest marriage, help couples who are remarrying and remarried finally get it right this time, and help married couples who are in a rut or in perpetual conflict to resolve their issues and spice up their marriages. Susan believes in everlasting love and that there is a mate for those who want one that aligns and connects with them at a soul level.

Through her compassionate, humorous, spiritual, and inspirational style, Susan coaches and educates singles and couples so they can learn the skills and tools they need to master the art of successful relationships and experience their own great love stories. Susan likes to take her clients to their deepest truths about themselves and their relationships or marriages and clear what's preventing them from experiencing the joys of love. Despite the divorce rate statistics being so high for first marriages and even higher for second and third marriages, Susan believes that with the right tools and skills, marriage can be a blissful experience and those divorce rates can drop!

With Susan as your coach, you will learn how to:

- Avoid the pitfalls of poor communication and learn to speak and be spoken to effectively, respectfully, and lovingly
- Uncover and release old issues, patterns, beliefs, and stories that are interfering in your relationship and blocking you from finding and allowing authentic love
- Utilize the tools and skills essential for relationship and marriage success that you never learned in school
- Experience what it feels like to come home to the love of your life and thoroughly enjoy it!
- Reignite and increase the intimacy that has fallen away over time
- Cope with the unexpected and challenging issues that present themselves over the course of a lifelong partnership
- Reignite and increase the intimacy that has fallen away over time
- Co-create and navigate your relationship as a team
- Experience more harmony through understanding how to resolve conflict with grace and dignity
- Learn the biggest secret to living your own happily-ever-after

Visit Susan's website for a virtual class schedule and on-line products. Contact Susan directly or apply for a seventy-five-minute complimentary consultation and relationship or marriage assessment if you are interested in private coaching.

Susan@ConsciousSoulMates.com
818-232-3186
www.ConsciousSoulMates.com

Book Susan Ortolano

TO SPEAK AT YOUR NEXT EVENT OR TO FACILITATE A WORKSHOP

When it comes to choosing a compassionate, funny, and knowledgeable speaker about marriage and relationships for your next event, you'll find Susan Ortolano can provide you with presentations and workshops that are not only educational, but compassionate, entertaining, and transformational for your audience, allowing them to see relationships and marriage through a new lens. As a Professional Certified & Seasoned Relationship and Marriage Coach with over a decade of experience, a Relationship Coach Trainer, an Award-Winning Educator, and a happily married lady, Susan will engage with your audience in a heartfelt, authentic way and lead them on a personal and soul-centered journey that anyone who has ever been in a romantic relationship can connect with. Her stories and content bring forward new and deeper levels of awareness, with inspiration, humor, vulnerability, and understanding, as well as a down-to-earth "get real" perspective on mastering the art of successful relationships.

Whether your audience is 10 or 10,000, Susan Ortolano will deliver a tailor-made message of love, authenticity, hope, and inspiration about relationships and marriage for your meeting, conference, event, or classroom. Susan feels that the most important area of life is *love*, and with the divorce rate statistics for first, second, and third marriages ranging from 45 percent up to 90 percent, she feels that everyone deserves to be in a happy and loving relationship, defying those statistics with the skills and tools finally to get love right! If you are seeking a memorable and unique speaker and you want your audience to learn the deeper truth about love, relationships, and marriage, then book Susan for your event today!

Sample Speaking Topics:

- **Remarrying Right:** Successfully Navigating the Uncharted Territory of Remarriage
- **Blending You, Me, Us & Them:** The Unique Dynamics of the Blended Family
- **Mastering the Art of Communication in Relationships:** Speaking Beyond the Cliché
- **Spicing Up Your Marriage:** Moving Beyond the Rut Through Wholistic Intimacy
- **Making Your Wedding Cake:** Understanding the Real Ingredients for a Successful Marriage
- **Understanding the Truth About Being Single:** What Needs to Happen to Manifest Marriage with Your Soul Mate and to Learn to Love Your Life
- **From Planning Your Wedding to Planning Your Marriage:** How to Make Yours Last After the Honeymoon Is Over

- **Moving from Conflict to Common Ground:** Resolving Conflict with Grace, Vulnerability, and Dignity
- **Coping With the Unexpected:** Marriage, Illness, Grief, and Loss
- **Marrying Out of the Box:** Thriving in Non-Traditional Marriages and Committed Relationships
- **Living on the Brink:** Deciding Whether to Stay Married or Get Divorced.
- **Reconciling Infidelity:** Uncovering the Truth About Infidelity and Whether or Not a Marriage Can Truly Recover

You can contact Susan for a complimentary pre-speech phone interview at 818-232-3186 or email her: Susan@ConsciousSoulMates.com